Chess Openings for Kids

John Watson and Graham Burgess

GRAND PRIX ATTACK

First published in the UK by Gambit Publications Ltd 2011
Reprinted 2013, 2014, 2017, 2021
Copyright © John Watson and Graham Burgess 2011

ISBN-13: 978-1-906454-26-5
ISBN-10: 1-906454-26-4

DISTRIBUTION:
Worldwide (except USA): Central Books Ltd, 50 Freshwater Road, Chadwell Heath, London RM8 1RX, England.
Tel +44 (0)20 8986 4854 Fax +44 (0)20 8533 5821. E-mail: orders@Centralbooks.com

Gambit Publications Ltd, 27 Queens Pine, Bracknell, Berks, RG12 0TL, England.
E-mail: info@gambitbooks.com
Website (regularly updated): www.gambitbooks.com

Edited by Graham Burgess
Typeset by Petra Nunn
All illustrations by Cindy McCluskey
Printed and bound by TJ Books Limited, Padstow, Cornwall, England

10 9 8 7 6 5

Gambit Publications Ltd
Directors: Dr John Nunn GM, Murray Chandler GM, and Graham Burgess FM
German Editor: Petra Nunn WFM
Bookkeeper: Andrea Burgess

Contents

FRIED LIVER ATTACK

Introduction

Let's face it: it's more fun to win a game of chess than lose, and no fun at all to lose quickly. In fact, there's nothing so frustrating as to sit down, make a few moves, and find out that your pieces are already disappearing and your king is getting chased around! Wouldn't it be nice to have your opponent on the run instead? The first moves of a chess game make up the *opening*, and the opening is often the trickiest and most important part of the game. This book gives you the knowledge you need to get off to a good start. It's not hard: you just need to know the principles of good opening play and get some practice with them.

We assume only that our readers know how to play chess, and are familiar with some of the basic tactics. This book follows the same structure as Murray Chandler's *How to Beat Your Dad at Chess* and *Chess Tactics for Kids*, and if you have read those books, you'll be especially well prepared to get to grips with some openings where you can put all those checkmate and tactical ideas to good use.

We're going to show you **50 Mighty Openings**. We call them that because they are the openings which have proven effective after thousands of games by masters over many years. So you can use these openings to win games not only when you're starting out, but also for as long as you play chess. We've chosen our examples to illustrate the most important strategies of chess play, strategies which also apply to later stages of the game. You will learn plenty of tactical ideas which every player should know, which means you can launch powerful attacks at the first opportunity, and be able to defend against impetuous raids by the enemy. Most of all, you'll have more fun playing as you take the next steps towards chess mastery. Enjoy this book and refer to it often!

SIBERIAN TRAP

Algebraic Notation

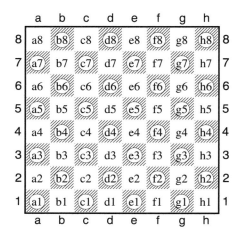

The chess notation used in this book is the simple, algebraic notation in use throughout the world. It can be learnt by anyone in just a few minutes.

As you can see from the chessboard above, the files are labelled a-h (going from left to right) and the ranks are labelled 1-8. This gives each square its own unique reference point. The pieces are described as follows:

Knight = ♘
Bishop = ♗
Rook = ♖
Queen = ♕
King = ♔

Pawns are not given a symbol. When they move, simply the *destination square* is given.

The following additional symbols are also used:

Check	=	+	Good move	=	!
Double Check	=	++	Bad move	=	?
Capture	=	x	Interesting idea	=	!?
Castles kingside	=	0-0	Not recommended	=	?!
Castles queenside	=	0-0-0	Brilliant move	=	!!
See diagram 2a (etc.)	=	*(2a)*	Disastrous move	=	??

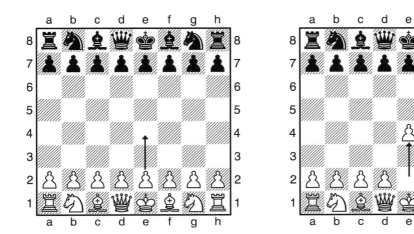

In the left-hand diagram above, White is about to play the move **1 e4**. The **1** indicates the move-number, and **e4** the destination square of the white pawn.

If we mention a move without giving a move-number, then it is an idea that might be played sooner or later depending on what the opponent does. If we put three dots before the move, this means it is an idea for Black.

In the right-hand diagram, White's **1 e4** move is complete. Black is about to reply **1...♘f6** (moving his knight to the **f6-square** on his *first move*).

To check you've got the hang of it, play through the following moves on your chessboard: 1 e4 e5 2 ♘f3 ♘c6 3 ♗b5 a6 4 ♗a4 ♘f6 5 0-0. You should now have the position shown in the right-hand diagram on page 34.

REVERSED DRAGON

7

How to Play the Opening

Development and the Centre

The first thing you have to do is get your pieces into play quickly. That means bringing the knights, bishops, queen and rooks into the fight, because they have greater range and can do more damage than the slow-moving pawns. But you can't get those pieces out (except for the knights) without first moving some pawns, so the basic idea of most good openings is to move one or two pawns and then get the other pieces into action. This is called *development*. Strong players will always tell you to develop your pieces before launching an attack. The special move castling is also important: it not only attends to the king's safety, but also develops a rook for future use.

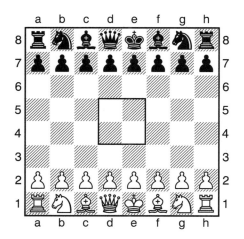

OK, but where should your pieces go? The important thing is to fight for the *centre*. The centre consists of the four squares shown in the diagram.

What's First?

From White's point of view, a formation with pawns standing side-by-side on the central squares d4 and e4 is called the *ideal centre*. If you've set up the ideal centre, your pieces will come out easily, without blocking each other. Take a look at the moves 1 e4 a5? 2 d4 h5? 3 ♘f3 d6 4 ♘c3 ♗d7 5 ♗c4 e6 6 0-0 ♘a6 7 ♗f4 ♘h6 8 ♕e2 g6 9 ♖ad1 h4 10 ♖fe1.

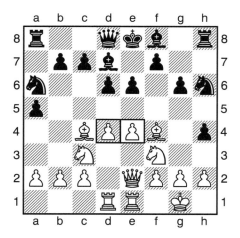

White has the ideal centre and all his pieces aim at the central squares. On the other hand, Black's bishops point away from the centre and his knights are on the side of the board. White can manoeuvre freely and is ready to attack in any part of the board.

This example points to a very important factor in the opening: the *activity* of your pieces. This means the range of squares that they can go to. In the diagram, White's pieces are all active, while Black's activity is sadly limited.

Don't Neglect Development

If you move your pawns too much and don't develop your pieces quickly, you will often get in trouble and even lose material. In the previous example, Black made six pawn moves and only three piece moves. Here's another example: 1 e4 e5 2 ♘c3 ♘f6 3 ♗c4 d6 4 ♘f3 c5? 5 ♘g5! h6? 6 ♘xf7, forking Black's queen and rook.

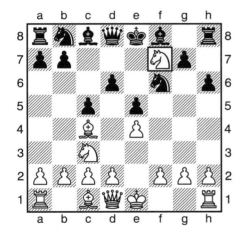

This is a standard attack on f7 that you will often see in beginners' games. Black made too many pawn moves and not enough piece moves.

Can we ever be 'pawn-pushers' and get away with throwing many of our pawns forward into battle right in the opening? Not usually, but if they help control central squares, a series of early pawn moves can be justified. Here's an example: 1 d4 ♘f6 2 c4 g6 3 ♘c3 ♗g7 4 e4 d6 5 f4 0-0 6 ♘f3.

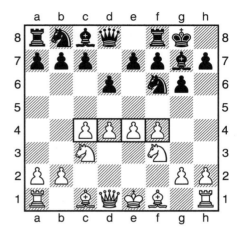

Black has developed two pieces and castled, and is now ready for battle in the centre. Meanwhile, White still needs to develop his king's bishop before he can castle. That could easily prove a problem for White, but his massive wall of pawns covers the key central squares multiple times, whereas Black has so far made only one little pawn move to contest e5. White also controls more *space*, which is an advantage in chess. Overall, you can say that although the two sides have applied different philosophies, both have played logically, and they are equally well-prepared for the game to come.

Gambits

In this book we take a look at quite a few *gambits*. These are openings in which White or Black gives up a pawn or two in order to achieve some of the important goals we have talked about: developing quickly, controlling the centre, or gaining good piece activity. Gambit openings are particularly well suited for the less-experienced player, because they can be easy to play, and being a pawn behind is not always that important at lower levels of competition. Examples of gambits are Mighty Openings 2, 4, 5, 6, 13, 23, 29, 34 and 39, as well as certain variations of other openings (which we'll point out).

Keep the King Safe!
Be careful before you move pawns that expose your king to attack. This particularly applies to the f-pawn:

1 f4 e5 2 fxe5 d6 3 exd6 ♗xd6

Black is playing a gambit, sacrificing a pawn for development and activity.

4 c4?? ♕h4+ 5 g3 ♗xg3+ 6 hxg3 ♕xg3#

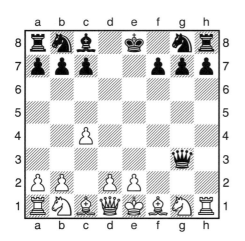

While White moved his f-pawn, exposing his king, and then lost time capturing his opponent's pawns, Black moved both his centre pawns, developed, and went after the defenceless enemy monarch.

Clear the Way
Knights and bishops are called *minor pieces* (as opposed to queens and rooks, which are called *major pieces*). Usually you'll want to bring your minor pieces out before your major pieces, like this:

1 e4 e5 2 ♘f3 ♘c6 3 ♗c4 ♗c5 4 d3 ♘f6

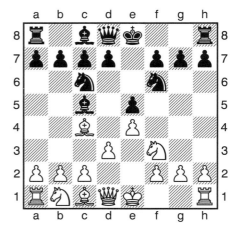

Both sides have moved centre pawns, and both sides have developed minor pieces. Good play. This clears the way for castling, which is the next step for both players:

5 0-0 0-0

In the vast majority of openings, both sides castle. Castling allows a rook to develop and makes the king safer. For example, with a king on g1 and pawns on f2, g2 and h2, Black can't put a piece on f3, g3 or h3 without it getting captured, while the sensitive f2-square is now protected by the rook on f1.

Connecting Rooks and Centralization
After castling and completing the development of your minor pieces, the next

thing is to get the major pieces (queen and rooks) into action. When you've castled and moved the queen and minor pieces off your own first rank, that's called *connecting the rooks*. Rooks need manoeuvring room on the back rank.

1 e4 c5 2 ♘f3 d6 3 d4 cxd4 4 ♘xd4 ♘f6 5 ♘c3 g6 6 ♗e3 ♗g7 7 f3 0-0 8 ♕d2 ♘c6 9 ♗c4 ♗d7 10 0-0-0 ♕a5

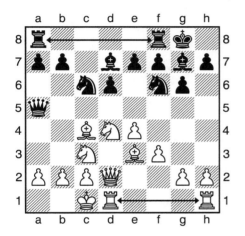

In this famous opening, called the Sicilian Dragon, both White and Black have brought out their minor pieces and queens, and they've castled. Their rooks are connected and ready for action.

Careful with Her Majesty

If you had an army, you wouldn't want the queen fighting on the front lines, because she's too valuable to lose. In chess, be careful not to expose your queen too early in the opening. Here's an example:

1 e4 d5 2 exd5 ♕xd5 3 ♘c3 ♕e5+? 4 ♗e2 ♘c6 5 ♘f3

For a second time, White brings out a knight while gaining time by attacking the

black queen. Making a developing move that forces a non-developing reply is called *developing with tempo*. It is an important concept that we shall see many times throughout this book.

5...♕a5 6 d4 ♗d7? 7 d5 ♘d8 8 ♘e5! ♘f6 9 ♘c4 ♕a6 10 ♗f4 e6

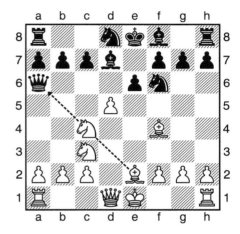

11 ♘d6+! ♗xd6 12 ♗xa6

Black's queen, which has moved four times, is lost for only two minor pieces.

Tips about Bishops and Knights

When you have two bishops on the board, and your opponent has traded one or both of his bishops off for a knight, we say that you have the *bishop-pair* or simply *two bishops*. Notice that the bishops together control squares of both colours. The side with two bishops often has an advantage over the side with fewer bishops, even if the material is equal. An exception arises when the knight sits on a square that can't be attacked by enemy pawns – this is called an *outpost*. A central outpost is particularly strong. Here's an example:

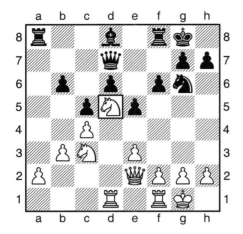

Black can't chase White's knight away from d5. The knight radiates power, and even if it's exchanged, another knight or a rook can take its place. Notice Black's poor bishop, blocked by its own pawns. This is called a *bad bishop*.

Weak Pawns

The *pawn-structure* that results from an opening can determine the course of the rest of the game. You should be careful to avoid making *weaknesses* in your pawn-structure, which can leave the pawns themselves vulnerable and/or allow the opponent's pieces to infiltrate around them. One example of a weakness is the *backward pawn*; such a pawn lags behind its neighbours and therefore can't be defended by another pawn. The previous example showed a backward pawn on d6. It is a problem because White can attack the pawn by putting rooks on the d-file and a knight on b5, forcing Black's pieces into passive defence. Furthermore, White can station pieces on the outpost in front of d6,

a very common occurrence in positions with backward pawns.

The same thing applies to the *isolated pawn*, which has no friendly pawns on neighbouring files at all. It can't be defended by other pawns, and a piece sitting right in front of it is hard to drive away.

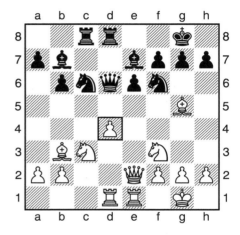

White's pawn on d4 is isolated. The pawn is defended for now, but it ties down two defenders (the knight on f3 and the rook on d1). Furthermore, Black has the square d5 as an outpost. After the move ...♞b4, for example, Black would have d5 covered six times, and a knight or bishop could settle comfortably on that fine square, not to be driven away.

Central isolated pawns aren't always bad, however, especially when there are still plenty of pieces on the board. In this case, White has more space (which means room to manoeuvre), and his pieces are active. Black has to watch out for the aggressive advance d5, and the move ♞e5 can put pressure on his position. Most strong players don't mind playing either side of middlegame positions with an isolated pawn in the centre. So we might say that such a pawn is both a weakness and a strength!

Finally, when a player has two pawns on the same file, they are called *doubled pawns*. These pawns are difficult to advance and can sometimes lead to other weaknesses in the pawn-structure. When doubled pawns are also isolated, they tend to be terribly weak.

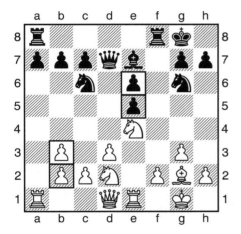

Black has doubled and isolated pawns on e5 and e6. The e4-square right in front of Black's doubled isolated pawns is an enemy outpost. White has a knight there, which is a great outpost piece, but you can see that any other piece on that square (a bishop, rook or queen – or even a king in an endgame!) would have excellent scope in several directions.

Notice that White has his own doubled pawns, on b2 and b3. But those pawns are

not isolated or vulnerable to attack, and there is no outpost square for Black's pieces. They also allow White's rook to operate on the a-file. Doubled pawns can be just as good as, or even better than, other pawns in your position, so don't be afraid of them. Later in the book, we shall even see some examples of doubled isolated pawns that turn out to be quite acceptable (see, e.g., page 31). Just try to avoid doubled pawns that offer weak points for your opponent to jump into.

So remember that not all backward, doubled or isolated pawns are harmful. But if we say that White (or Black) has a *bad pawn-structure*, that means that his pawn-weaknesses have the potential to cause him real problems.

What's Next?

As you go through the 50 openings in this book, you'll see the principles and ideas we've just discussed appearing again and again. Be patient – it takes some time to learn how to put them together in correct proportion. You'll also see cases where one player appears to abandon the principles in search of strategic or material gains – and goes unpunished! That's because in chess, concrete analysis can outweigh general principles, and this is one reason why chess is such a difficult game to master. But even a simple concentration upon the most important goals – central squares, development and activity – will often be enough to give you a big advantage right off the bat, and you'll gain some surprisingly quick victories.

Going for broke in the centre

The Italian Game, **1 e4 e5 2 ♘f3 ♘c6 3 ♗c4**, is a direct attempt to attack Black before he can get organized. There are tricks and traps galore, which makes it a great opening for attackers. In the Giuoco Piano, Black replies **3...♗c5** *(1a)*. Notice that the weak squares f7 and f2 are both targeted, so watch out for attacks on those squares. The main line runs **4 c3 ♘f6 5 d4 exd4 6 cxd4 ♗b4+ 7 ♗d2 ♗xd2+ 8 ♘bxd2 d5!** *(1b)*. White sets up the ideal centre, and Black blocks its advance, breaking it up. Contrast this with Diagram 2, where Black retreats with 6...♗b6? and White's pawns charge forward. White can also attack immediately with 6 e5, but Black plays 6...d5! (a theme to remember) 7 ♗b5 ♘e4, when 8 ♘xd4?! 0-0! 9 ♗xc6 bxc6 10 ♗e3 ♖e8 *(3)* is awkward for White. Instead, 4 d3 d6 5 0-0 ♘f6 *(4)* is a solid choice. But after the innocent-looking 6 ♗g5?! h6 7 ♗h4?! g5 8 ♗g3 h5! 9 ♘xg5?! h4! 10 ♘xf7 *(5)*, it's Black who has all the fun.

Basic Positions of the Giuoco Piano

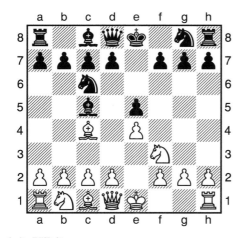

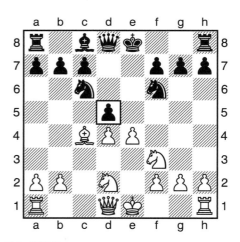

1a) White moves

White usually builds up his centre by 4 c3 ♘f6 5 d4. This forces lines open, since if Black simply retreats, the white pawns will advance further, scattering the black pieces in all directions.

1b) White moves

Black strikes back in the centre. After 9 exd5 ♘xd5, White's pawn on d4 is isolated, but he has more pieces out. It will be a battle between Black's better structure and White's active piece-play.

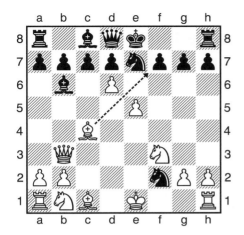

2) Black moves

This arises when Black plays 6...♗b6? and gets driven back: 7 d5 ♘e7 8 e5 ♘g4 9 d6 ♘xf2 10 ♕b3!. Now a possible finish is 10...♘g6? 11 ♗xf7+ ♔f8 12 ♗g5!, trapping and winning the black queen.

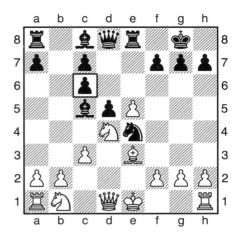

3) White moves

Can't White win a pawn by 11 ♘xc6 here? No, because 11...♗xe3!! 12 ♘xd8 ♗xf2+ wins the queen back with bonus material after either 13 ♔f1 ♗a6+ or 13 ♔e2 ♗g4+. Rapid development triumphs!

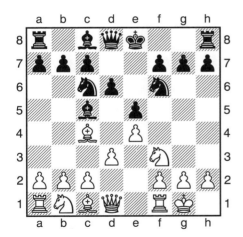

4) White moves

This is the Giuoco Pianissimo ('very quiet game'). Something like 6 h3 h6 7 a3 0-0 8 ♘c3 can follow. Both sides have solid pawn-structures and there's nothing much going on yet.

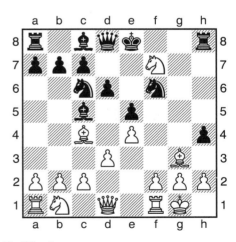

5) Black moves

Pure chaos! Black looks busted, but he sacrifices his queen by 10...hxg3!? 11 ♘xd8 ♗g4 12 ♕d2 ♘d4! 13 h3 ♘e2+, when 14 ♔h1?? ♖xh3+! 15 gxh3 ♗f3# is a beautiful finish (for Black, at least!).

15

Evans Gambit

Nothing ventured, nothing gained: Romantic chess at its best

The Evans Gambit was one of the most popular openings in the 19th century, and has enjoyed a modern revival. It arises after **1 e4 e5 2 ♘f3 ♘c6 3 ♗c4 ♗c5 4 b4** *(1a)*. White sacrifices a pawn, gaining time to construct an ideal centre and develop quickly. A traditional main line is 4...♗xb4 5 c3 ♗a5 6 d4 exd4 7 0-0 d6 8 cxd4 ♗b6 9 ♘c3 *(1b)*. This can explode into tactics. In Diagram 2, Black has varied with the safer 7...♘ge7, returning a pawn in order to achieve the counterblow ...d5. But there is a no-holds-barred fight ahead. The Lasker Defence is 6...d6 7 0-0 ♗b6 *(3)* (or 6 0-0 d6 7 d4 ♗b6). Black gives back the pawn to develop in safety and achieve a superior pawn-structure. Black can also accept the gambit and then return the pawn by 4...♗xb4 5 c3 ♗e7 6 d4 ♘a5 7 ♘xe5 (7 ♗e2 is more aggressive) 7...♘xc4 8 ♘xc4 *(4)*, hoping that his bishop-pair will be effective. Finally, Black can decline the gambit altogether by 4...♗b6 *(5)*.

Basic Positions of the Evans Gambit

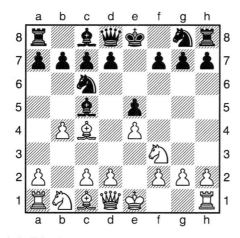

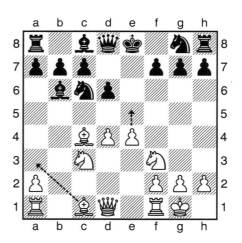

1a) Black moves

When Black captures the b-pawn with 4...♗xb4, White takes over the centre by 5 c3 ♗a5 6 d4, setting the deadly trap 6...♘f6? 7 dxe5 ♘xe4? 8 ♕d5, which threatens both 9 ♕xf7# and 9 ♕xe4.

1b) Black moves

If Black plays 9...♘f6?, White blasts away by 10 e5! dxe5 11 ♗a3!. Now Black can't castle, and 12 ♕b3 or 12 ♘g5 can follow, with a terrific attack. 9...♘a5 and 9...♗g4 are much tougher defences.

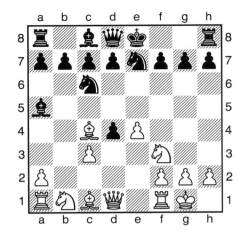

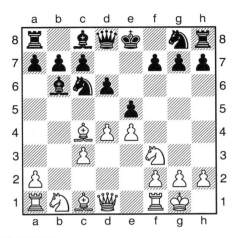

2) White moves

If White attacks by 8 ♘g5, he runs into 8...d5 9 exd5 ♘e5!. Black can also hold the centre following 8 cxd4 d5 9 exd5 ♘xd5 10 ♕b3 ♗e6! planning to meet 11 ♕xb7?! with 11...♘db4!, threatening 12...♖b8.

3) White moves

After 8 dxe5 dxe5 9 ♕xd8+ ♘xd8 10 ♘xe5 White's weak c3-pawn gives him a poor pawn-structure. Instead, 9 ♕b3 ♕f6 10 ♗g5 ♕g6 lets Black keep his extra pawn in return for some pressure.

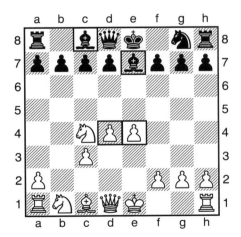

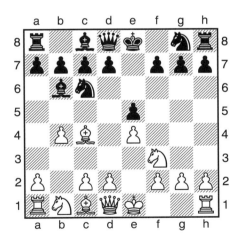

4) Black moves

Here Black can claim some space by 8...d5 9 exd5 ♕xd5 10 ♘e3 ♕a5. This should give roughly equal chances for the two sides, with White's better centre compensating for Black's bishop-pair.

5) White moves

After 5 b5 ♘a5 6 ♘xe5? ♘h6! Black threatens ...♗d4, ...d6 and ...♕g5. White does better with 5 a4 (intending 6 a5 to trap Black's bishop!), when 5...a6! 6 ♘c3 ♘f6 gives both sides chances.

Two Knights Defence

The best things come in pairs

The Two Knights Defence features **1 e4 e5 2 ♘f3 ♘c6 3 ♗c4**, and now **3...♘f6** *(1a)*. Black attacks the pawn on e4 and prepares ...d5, an effective central stroke. Notice that the natural move 4 ♘c3 can be met by the fork trick 4...♘xe4! 5 ♘xe4 d5. A direct test of the Two Knights is 4 ♘g5, attacking f7. After 4...d5 5 exd5, Black has several options. The main line is 5...♘a5 6 ♗b5+ c6 7 dxc6 bxc6 *(1b)*, when 8 ♗e2 is the traditional move. White can also play 8 ♗d3!?, taking control of e4, or 8 ♕f3 *(2)*, pinning the c6-pawn. If Black plays the obvious recapture 5...♘xd5?!, White can try the piece sacrifice 6 ♘xf7!? *(3)*, called the Fried Liver Attack. The wild Max Lange Attack continues 4 d4 exd4 5 0-0 (5 e5 runs into 5...d5!) 5...♗c5 6 e5 d5 7 exf6 dxc4 *(4)*. If Black grabs a centre pawn by 5...♘xe4 6 ♖e1 d5, the spectacular tactic 7 ♗xd5! *(5)* wins it back.

Basic Positions of the Two Knights Defence

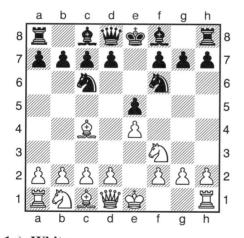

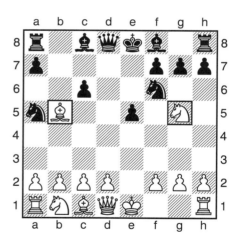

1a) White moves

Black is attacking e4, and if White simply defends the pawn, then Black will develop comfortably. The main line of the opening is a dramatic sequence beginning with 4 ♘g5 d5, where Black sacrifices a pawn to drive White back.

1b) White moves

Black gains time by attacking the loose white pieces in lines like 8 ♗e2 h6 9 ♘f3 e4 10 ♘e5 ♕c7. White is a pawn up, but Black has better development and central control. 8 ♗d3!? avoids some of these problems, but blocks the d-pawn.

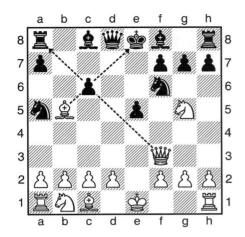

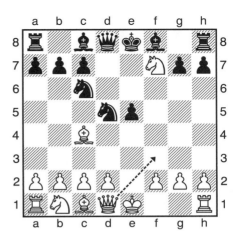

2) Black moves

8...♖b8! gives up a second pawn. 9 ♗xc6+
♘xc6 10 ♕xc6+ ♘d7 11 d3 ♗e7 12 ♘e4
♖b6 13 ♕a4 ♗b7 gives Black fast development, central control, the bishop-pair
and an attack in return for the pawns.

3) Black moves

The Fried Liver Attack. White's point is
6...♔xf7 7 ♕f3+ ♔e6 (risky, but the king
must defend his knight) 8 ♘c3 ♘e7 (or
8...♘b4!?) 9 d4!, when White is a piece
behind, but has a dangerous attack.

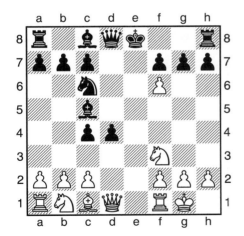

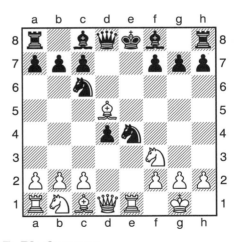

4) White moves

Tactics dominate! A nerve-wracking line
featuring a series of pins goes 8 ♖e1+ ♗e6
9 ♘g5 ♕d5! 10 ♘c3! ♕f5 11 ♘ce4 0-0-0
12 g4! ♕e5!, with bewildering complications. 9 fxg7 ♖g8 10 ♗g5 is another story.

5) Black moves

White will recover his piece due to the
double pin after 7...♕xd5 8 ♘c3!. But
Black can shrug this off with 8...♕h5 9
♘xe4 ♗e6, blocking White's attack down
the e-file.

King's Gambit

Method behind the madness, or simply crazy?

The King's Gambit arises after **1 e4 e5 2 f4** *(1a)*. This strange-looking move gives up a pawn and exposes White's king! But if Black accepts the gambit by 2...exf4, White gets the greater share of the centre with 3 ♘f3, intending a quick d4. He also plans to attack down the f-file. Black will often defend the pawn with 3...g5, and White tries to destroy his pawn-chain by 4 h4 g4 5 ♘e5 *(1b)*. The wild Muzio Gambit goes 3...g5 4 ♗c4 g4 (4...♗g7 is solid and safer) 5 0-0! gxf3 6 ♕xf3. White gives up a whole piece to attack down the f-file. A typical slugfest follows 6...♕f6 7 e5! ♕xe5 8 ♗xf7+! ♔xf7 9 d4 *(2)*. In the Modern Variation, Black returns the pawn for development: 3...d5 4 exd5 ♘f6 *(3)*. The Falkbeer Counter-Gambit is 2...d5 3 exd5 e4?! *(3...c6!? is another gambit approach, but similar to the Modern Variation)*, when 4 d3! ♘f6 5 dxe4 ♘xe4 6 ♘f3 *(4)* is a main line. Black can also decline the King's Gambit with 2...♗c5 *(5)* and get a solid position.

Basic Positions of the King's Gambit

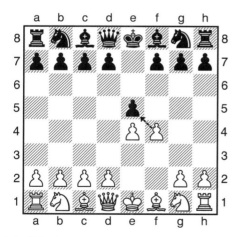

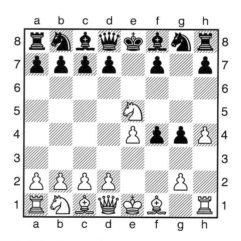

1a) Black moves

White attacks e5. By giving up a pawn, he wants to divert Black from control of d4, take over the centre, and launch an attack! Black is normally pleased to take up the offer by 2...exf4.

1b) Black moves

The simplest defence here is 5...♘f6. For example, 6 ♗c4 d5! or 6 d4 d6 7 ♘d3 ♘xe4 8 ♗xf4 ♕e7 9 ♗e2 ♘c6 (or 9...♗g7), when Black has an extra pawn in return for a slightly loose position.

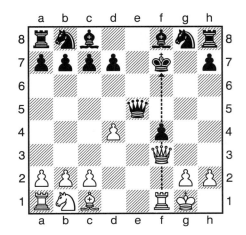

2) Black moves

White keeps giving: 9...♕xd4+ 10 ♗e3! ♕f6 11 ♘c3 planning ♕h5+, ♘d5 and ♗xf4. On the other hand, Black is two pieces ahead, so if he can hang on, it's all over for White!

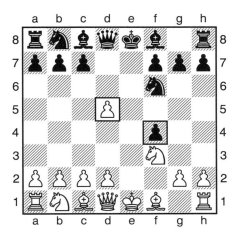

3) White moves

The sharp variation 5 ♗b5+ c6 6 dxc6 ♘xc6 7 d4 ♗d6 leaves Black's f-pawn alive, cramping White's pieces. But in return White owns more of the centre. 5 ♗c4 ♘xd5 6 0-0 is a simpler approach.

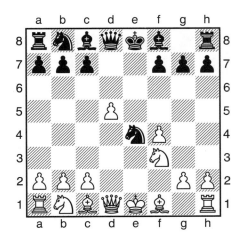

4) Black moves

6...♗c5 attacks f2, but the forcing 7 ♕e2 ♗f5 8 ♘c3 ♕e7 9 ♗e3! is good, since 9...♘xc3 10 ♗xc5! ♘xe2 11 ♗xe7 ♘xf4 12 ♗a3 ♘xd5 13 0-0-0 leaves Black's king stuck in the centre.

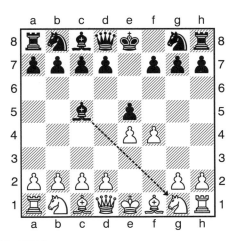

5) White moves

Now White must avoid playing 3 fxe5?? ♕h4+ 4 g3 ♕xe4+. After 3 ♘f3 d6 4 ♘c3 (or 4 c3!? intending d4) 4...♘f6 5 ♗c4 ♘c6 6 d3 ♗g4, Black's control of d4 balances out White's potential attack.

21

Danish Gambit and Centre Game

You have to risk something to get something

1 e4 e5 2 d4 exd4 3 c3 *(1a)* is the outrageous Danish Gambit. After 3...dxc3, White sacrifices a second pawn by 4 ♗c4!? (4 ♘xc3 ♘c6 5 ♘f3 is the Göring Gambit – see page 24) 4...cxb2 5 ♗xb2, to obtain two monstrous bishops aiming at Black's kingside. Slow moves like 5...d6 6 ♘c3 ♘f6 7 ♕b3! ♕e7 8 ♘f3 ♘c6 9 0-0-0 *(2)* allow White dangerous play. Black's most dynamic reply is the central counterattack 5...d5!?, intending the tricky 6 ♗xd5 ♘f6 *(3)*. Black is ready to capture the bishop on d5, but has he missed something? A good way to decline the gambit is 3...d5 4 exd5 ♕xd5 5 cxd4 ♘c6 *(4)*.

The Centre Game features **1 e4 e5 2 d4 exd4 3 ♕xd4** *(1b)*. The white queen is exposed in the middle of the board, like Black's queen in the Scandinavian Defence (page 44), so the question is if she can find a useful, secure and active post. The main line involves opposite-side castling: 3...♘c6 4 ♕e3 ♘f6 5 ♘c3 ♗b4 6 ♗d2 0-0 7 0-0-0 *(5)*.

Basic Positions of the Danish Gambit and Centre Game

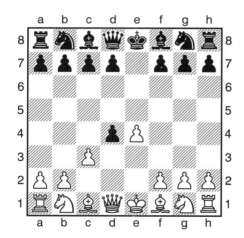

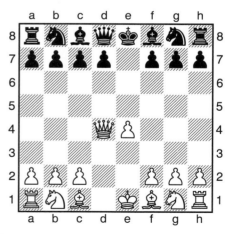

1a) Black moves

After 3...dxc3 4 ♗c4!? cxb2 5 ♗xb2, Black is two pawns ahead but has to deal with White's active bishops, control of the centre, and threats against f7 and g7. That requires careful defence.

1b) Black moves

White has more space. Black can activate his bishop by 3...♘c6 4 ♕e3 g6 5 ♘c3 ♗g7 6 ♗d2 ♘f6 7 0-0-0 0-0 8 ♗c4, when 8...♖e8 puts direct pressure on e4 in return for White's freer game.

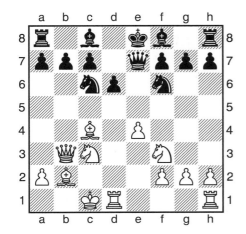

2) Black moves

White's centralized development makes it easy for Black to go wrong. 9...♖b8? 10 ♖he1! ♗e6? 11 e5! dxe5 12 ♘xe5 ♘xe5 13 ♖xe5 followed by ♗xe6 is an example of the sort of thing Black must avoid.

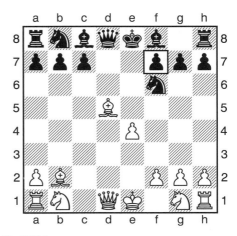

3) White moves

7 ♗xf7+ ♔xf7 8 ♕xd8 wins the queen, but Black calmly regains it by 8...♗b4+ 9 ♕d2 ♗xd2+ 10 ♘xd2. Another trick is 7 ♘c3 ♘xd5 8 ♘xd5 c6? (8...♘d7 is better) 9 ♘f6+! gxf6 10 ♕xd8+ ♔xd8 11 ♗xf6+.

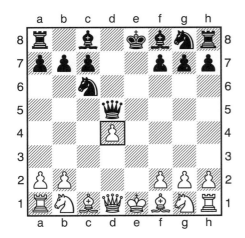

4) White moves

Black returns the pawn and threatens to capture on d4. A popular line goes 6 ♘f3 ♗g4 7 ♗e2 ♗b4+ 8 ♘c3 ♗xf3 9 ♗xf3 ♕c4!, preventing White from castling and attacking c3. 6 ♗e3!? avoids the ...♗g4 pin.

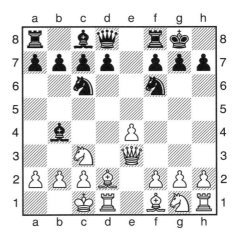

5) Black moves

Opposite-side castling generally produces attacking chess: 7...♖e8 8 ♕g3! prevents 8...♗xc3 9 ♗xc3 ♘xe4?? due to 10 ♕xg7#. Black can play 8...♖xe4! instead, with great complications.

Göring and Latvian Gambits

Keep the pressure on... or else!

The Göring Gambit, **1 e4 e5 2 ♘f3 ♘c6 3 d4 exd4 4 c3** *(1a)*, resembles the Danish Gambit, but White sacrifices only one pawn to get developed. If Black accepts by 4...dxc3 5 ♘xc3, he has to decide how to protect against a straightforward attack by ♗c4 and ♕b3 or ♘g5. One way is 5...d6 6 ♗c4 and now 6...♗e6 *(2)* or 6...♘f6 7 ♕b3 ♕d7! (intending ...♘a5) 8 ♘g5 ♘e5 *(3)*. With another sequence, 5...♗b4 6 ♗c4 d6 *(4)*, Black tries to develop the king's bishop and get castled quickly. We should note that Black can decline in just the same way as we saw against the Danish Gambit: 4...d5 5 exd5 ♕xd5 6 cxd4 reaches a position we examined on page 23.

After **1 e4 e5 2 ♘f3**, Black can gambit a pawn as early as move 2 with the bold **2...f5?!** *(1b)*. This is called the Latvian Gambit, and it resembles the King's Gambit, with some of the same ideas. One important line goes 3 ♘xe5 ♕f6 4 d4 d6 5 ♘c4 fxe4 6 ♘c3 *(5)*.

Basic Positions of the Göring and Latvian Gambits

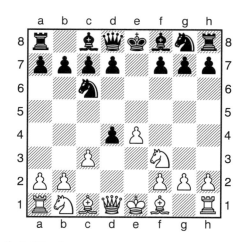

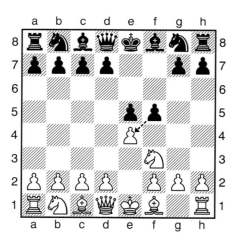

1a) Black moves

White offers a pawn to open lines in the centre and bring his pieces out quickly and actively. If Black takes on c3, White will have firm control over the centre, preventing Black's ...d5 advance.

1b) White moves

Black immediately attacks e4. By contrast with the King's Gambit, if White accepts the pawn by 3 exf5, Black has the immediate attack 3...e4, advancing with the gain of a tempo.

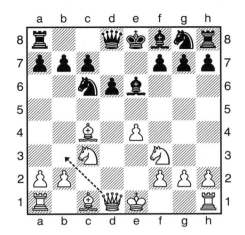

2) White moves

White should keep the initiative by 7 ♗xe6 fxe6 8 ♕b3 attacking b7 and e6; for example, 8...♕c8 9 ♘g5 ♘d8 10 f4 with the idea of e5 or f5. Black has an extra pawn, but is cramped.

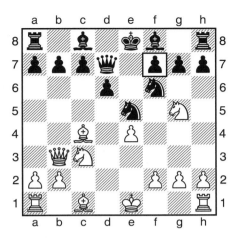

3) White moves

The f7-square is defended and Black will play ...h6 next. White can't afford to lose time, so he tries 9 ♗b5 c6 10 f4! cxb5 11 fxe5 dxe5 12 ♗e3 intending ♖d1 with a typical attack for two pawns.

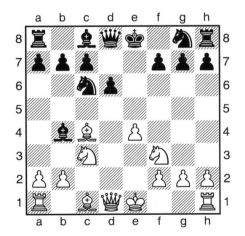

4) White moves

If the game goes 7 0-0 ♗xc3 8 bxc3 ♘f6, then White, to stop ...0-0, can try the radical 9 e5!? ♘xe5 10 ♘xe5 dxe5 11 ♕b3 ♕e7 12 ♗a3 c5 13 ♗b5+ with great complications.

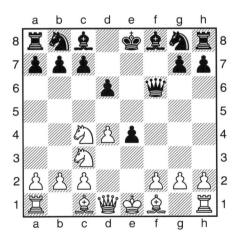

5) Black moves

White has a real lead in development, while Black wants to use his e4-pawn to cramp White. One possible continuation is 6...♕g6 7 f3 exf3 8 ♕xf3 ♘f6 9 ♗d3 with some advantage for White.

7 Bishop's Opening and Vienna Game

Old-fashioned development

These are two older openings that are still good weapons. The Bishop's Opening, **1 e4 e5 2 ♗c4** *(1a)*, develops and controls d5. On the downside, it doesn't attack e5 like 2 ♘f3 does. The main line after 2 ♗c4 goes 2...♘f6 3 d3 c6 4 ♘f3 d5 *(2)*, advancing in the centre with tempo. In this line, Black can also break immediately with 3...d5?! 4 exd5 ♘xd5, when White can gain some central initiative after 5 ♘f3 ♘c6 6 0-0 ♗e7 7 ♖e1 *(3)*. The Vienna Game, **1 e4 e5 2 ♘c3** *(1b)*, is similar to the Bishop's Opening in that White develops a piece and controls d5. 2...♘f6 is the most popular and aggressive response. One key idea is that after 3 ♗c4, Black has the trick 3...♘xe4! *(4)*, which can get extremely complicated. 3 f4 looks like a King's Gambit, but 3...d5! *(5)* is an effective counter (not 3...exf4? 4 e5). White can also play 3 ♘f3, when 3...♘c6 is called the Four Knights Game. We look at 4 d4 on page 28, while 4 ♗b5 can be met by 4...♘d4!?.

Basic Positions of the Bishop's Opening and Vienna Game

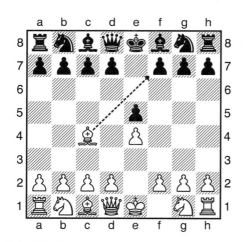

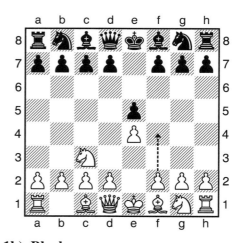

1a) Black moves

White develops and takes immediate aim at f7. The choice between ♘f3 and f4 is left open for the time being. In the absence of immediate threats, Black has freedom to operate in the centre.

1b) Black moves

In the Vienna Game, White covers d5, protects e4 and avoids giving Black a target. One idea is that the move f4, as in the King's Gambit, is still possible. But Black has time to respond actively in the centre.

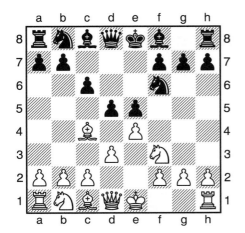

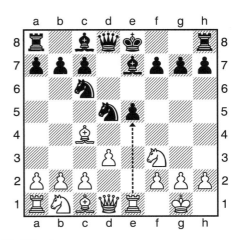

2) White moves

Black has taken his share of the centre, but White is content with 5 ♗b3!, which has the point 5...dxe4?! 6 ♘g5!. Instead, 5...♗d6 6 ♘c3 dxe4 7 ♘xe4 ♘xe4 8 dxe4 0-0 is normal.

3) Black moves

White is attacking Black's e-pawn with his knight and rook. After the natural defence, 7...f6?!, White plays 8 d4!, when it's difficult to keep Black's centre intact. 7...♗g4 8 h3 ♗h5 9 g4 ♗g6 is a gambit.

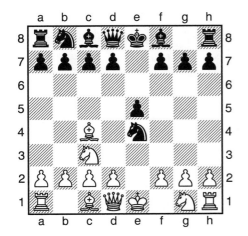

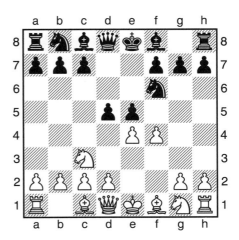

4) White moves

After 4 ♘xe4 d5 Black wins back the piece. White also has the clever 4 ♕h5! (attacking f7) 4...♘d6 5 ♗b3 ♘c6 (safer is 5...♗e7) 6 ♘b5! (threatening ♘xd6+) 6...g6 7 ♕f3 f5, with wild, unclear play.

5) White moves

Black opens lines and threatens the e4-pawn. A natural line is 4 fxe5 ♘xe4 5 ♘f3 ♗c5! 6 d4 ♗b4 7 ♗d2 c5, undermining White's centre. 4 exd5 e4! 5 ♕e2 ♗e7 is an improved Falkbeer (page 20).

27

Scotch Game

Seize territory, but be prepared to defend it!

By playing the Scotch Game, **1 e4 e5 2 ♘f3 ♘c6 3 d4 exd4 4 ♘xd4** *(1a)*, White gains space and opens lines. On the other hand, if Black now plays 4...♘f6, he will already be ahead in development, and attacking the e4-pawn. This gives White two main options. He can bring out a piece by 5 ♘c3 (this is the Scotch Four Knights – 1 e4 e5 2 ♘f3 ♘c6 3 ♘c3 ♘f6 4 d4 exd4 5 ♘xd4 also reaches this position). After 5...♗b4 6 ♘xc6 bxc6 7 ♗d3, White's e4-pawn is defended, but 7...d5! 8 exd5 cxd5 9 0-0 0-0 *(3)* gives Black his share of the centre. Or White can play 5 ♘xc6 bxc6 6 e5 *(1b)*, trying to dislodge the knight from f6. This can lead directly to the intense and popular position in Diagram 2. Black's other main move against the Scotch is 4...♗c5, developing a piece with an attack on d4. Then 5 ♗e3 ♕f6! 6 c3 ♘ge7 *(4)* is double-edged, while after 5 ♘xc6, the tricky 5...♕f6! *(5)* prepares to recapture the knight without having to exchange queens.

Basic Positions of the Scotch Game

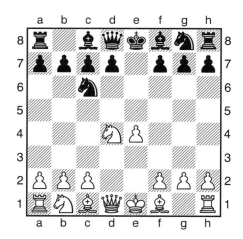

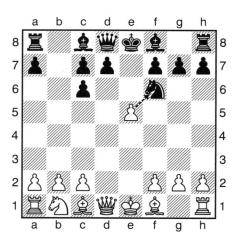

1a) Black moves

The Scotch Game. White wants to play principled moves like ♗c4, 0-0 and ♘c3, but Black will disrupt things before they get that far. He is a little short of space but can get his pieces out quickly.

1b) Black moves

Now Black shouldn't go backwards with 6...♘g8, and 6...♘d5 7 c4 is uncomfortable. So the main line is 6...♕e7 7 ♕e2 ♘d5 8 c4 ♗a6. Then 9 b3 *(2)* both protects c4 and prepares ♗b2.

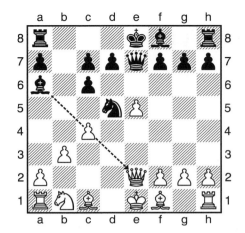

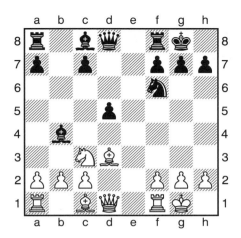

2) Black moves

Black fianchettoes his bishop by 9...g5 or 9...g6 and ...♗g7. With so many loose pieces, both sides must watch out for early tactics, but once White has developed, he will enjoy the better structure.

3) White moves

Black can play ...c6 next with a solid position. There are some little tricks here like 10 ♗g5 ♗e7?! 11 ♗xf6 ♗xf6 12 ♘xd5! ♕xd5?? (12...♗xb2 is correct) 13 ♗xh7+ and White wins the queen!

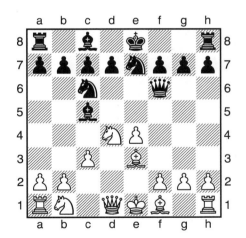

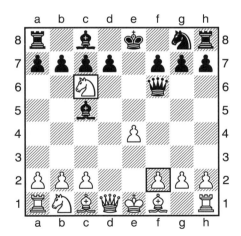

4) White moves

Now 7 ♗c4 develops a piece and prevents ...d5. Then after 7...♘e5, 8 ♗e2 loses a pawn to 8...♕g6, forking e4 and g2. However, 9 0-0 ♕xe4 10 ♘d2 leaves Black facing quite an attack.

5) White moves

Black leaves the knight hanging for a moment as he threatens mate on f2. Now a clever move is 6 ♕d2!, which allows White's bishop on f1 to develop quickly. Both sides have chances here.

MIGHTY OPENING **9** Philidor Defence

Black builds a fortress

1 e4 e5 2 ♘f3 d6 *(1a)* is the Philidor Defence. Black supports his e5-pawn, but 3 d4 gives White the lion's share of the centre. 3...exd4 opens the game and after 4 ♘xd4 ♘f6 5 ♘c3 g6 6 ♗c4 ♗g7 *(5)* Black seeks play on the long diagonal. After 3...♘d7, the natural sequence 4 ♘c3 ♘gf6 5 ♗c4 ♗e7 6 0-0 0-0 *(1b)* reaches the traditional main-line position. However, White can play 4 ♗c4!, with some clever tricks in mind, stemming from 4...♘gf6? 5 dxe5! ♘xe5 6 ♘xe5 dxe5 *(2)* or 4...♗e7? 5 dxe5 ♘xe5 (5...dxe5?? loses to 6 ♕d5!) 6 ♘xe5 dxe5 *(3)*. To avoid these problems, a modern way of playing the Philidor is 1 e4 d6 2 d4 ♘f6 3 ♘c3 (so far an opening called the Pirc Defence, where the normal plan is a fianchetto with 3...g6 and later action in the centre) 3...e5. The point is that 4 ♘f3 ♘bd7 will lead to positions like Diagram 1b while avoiding the tricks in Diagrams 2 and 3. Simplifying by 4 dxe5 dxe5 5 ♕xd8+ ♔xd8 6 ♗c4 *(4)* gives White little.

Basic Positions of the Philidor Defence

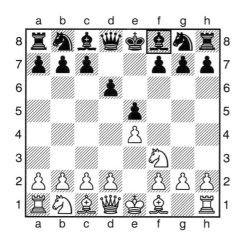

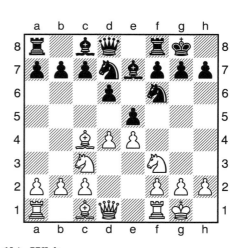

1a) White moves

Black has protected e5, but hemmed in his bishop on f8. After 3 d4, Black can either support a strongpoint on e5 or play ...exd4 and ...g6 in order to gain activity. There's also the aggressive 3...f5?!.

1b) White moves

After 7 ♕e2 c6, Black intends ...b5, and 8 a4 ♕c7 9 ♖d1 b6 can follow, with the idea ...♗b7. White has more space, but it will be hard to break down Black's fortress. Both sides have many options.

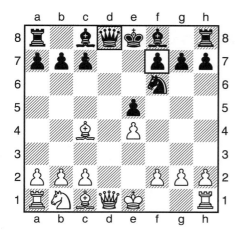

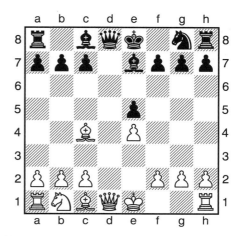

2) White moves

White has a trick which is familiar from the Danish Gambit: 7 ♗xf7+! ♔xf7 8 ♕xd8. Although Black regains the queen by 8...♗b4+ 9 ♕d2 ♗xd2+ 10 ♘xd2, here White is a clear pawn ahead.

3) White moves

Here too White wins material by using a simple fork: 7 ♕h5! g6 8 ♕xe5. Black has to be very careful in these lines, a fact which has led him to try other move-orders, most notably 1 e4 d6!

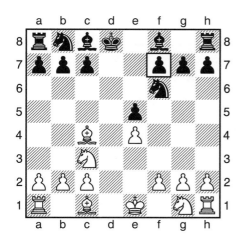

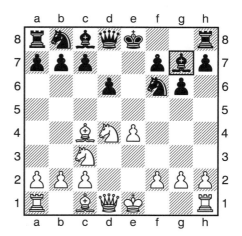

4) Black moves

Black's position remains solid after 6...♔e8. He can also accept doubled isolated pawns by 6...♗e6 7 ♗xe6 fxe6, since these pawns control important central squares and are hard to attack.

5) White moves

Black gives up central control to White, intending to exert pressure on the long h8-a1 diagonal. Play can continue 7 f3 0-0 8 ♗e3 with the idea ♕d2 and 0-0-0, which resembles a Sicilian Dragon (page 64).

Petroff Defence

Copycat tactics with counterattacking twists

In the Petroff, Black answers **1 e4 e5 2 ♘f3** with **2...♘f6** *(1a)*, attacking the e4-pawn. Beginners are warned about the danger of copying White's moves, and shown horror stories like 3 ♘xe5 ♘xe4?! 4 ♕e2 ♘f6?? (4...♕e7 5 ♕xe4 d6 is better) 5 ♘c6+, winning the black queen. But the Petroff is a respectable opening because Black meets 3 ♘xe5 with 3...d6! before ...♘xe4. In lines like 3 d4 ♘xe4 (3...d5 is possible too!) 4 ♗d3 d5 5 ♘xe5 *(2a)*, the game doesn't stay symmetrical for long either. After 3 ♘xe5 d6 4 ♘f3 ♘xe4, the question is how ambitious White is feeling. 5 d3 ♘f6 6 d4 d5 is actually an Exchange French (page 48), and 5 ♕e2 ♕e7 6 d3 ♘f6 leads to a dull ending – a problem if Black desperately wants to win! The main lines are 5 ♘c3 ♘xc3 6 dxc3 *(3)* and 5 d4 d5 *(1b)*, which looks like an Exchange French with a free move for Black. But White will attack the e4-knight, and if he forces ...♘f6, then *White* will have won a move! Those who prefer to attack more directly may like the gambit 3 ♗c4 ♘xe4 4 ♘c3 *(4)*.

Basic Positions of the Petroff Defence

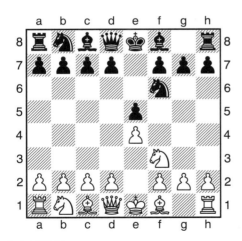

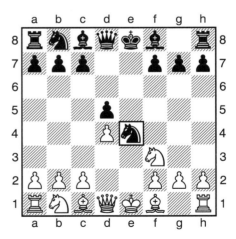

1a) White moves

White normally opens the game with 3 ♘xe5 or 3 d4, since 3 d3 ♘c6 followed by ...d5 is easy for Black, while 3 ♘c3 ♘c6 is a Four Knights (see page 26).

1b) White moves

6 ♗d3 ♗e7 7 0-0 ♘c6 8 c4 puts pressure on the knight. 8...♘b4 9 ♗e2 0-0 10 ♘c3 ♗f5 avoids a time-wasting retreat, but 11 a3 gives White the freer game.

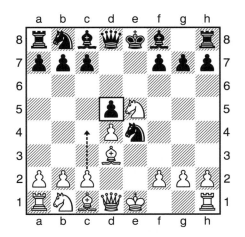

2a) Black moves

5...♗d6 6 0-0 0-0 7 c4 keeps the pressure on, as 7...♗xe5 8 dxe5 ♘c6 9 cxd5 ♕xd5 10 ♕c2 shows. 5...♘d7 gives Black more activity after 6 ♘xd7 ♗xd7 7 0-0 (2b), and 6 ♘xf7 ♕e7!? is sharp.

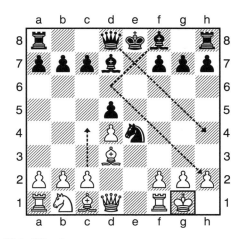

2b) Black moves

7...♕h4 8 c4 0-0-0 9 c5 leads to dramatic play, with both kings under fire. 7...♗d6 offers a pawn for activity: 8 c4 c6 9 cxd5 cxd5 10 ♕h5 0-0 11 ♕xd5 ♗c6. Note that 8 ♖e1 ♗xh2+ 9 ♔xh2 ♕h4+ draws.

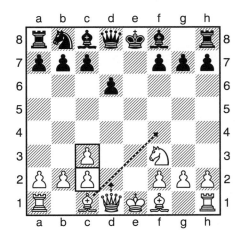

3) Black moves

Rather than worry about pawn-structure, White intends to develop quickly and launch an attack against the black king. His own king will sit securely on c1 after 6...♗e7 7 ♗f4 0-0 8 ♕d2 ♘d7 9 0-0-0.

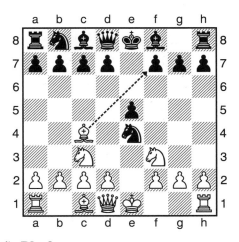

4) Black moves

White has very active play after 4...♘xc3 5 dxc3; e.g., 5...f6 (not 5...d6? 6 ♘g5 ♗e6 7 ♗xe6 fxe6 8 ♕f3) 6 ♘h4 g6 7 f4 intending f5. But Black can decline the pawn by 4...♘c6!, based on 5 ♘xe4 d5.

33

Ruy Lopez: Introduction

The opening that has stood the test of time like no other

The Ruy Lopez is one of the oldest and most important openings. After **1 e4 e5 2 ♘f3 ♘c6**, White plays **3 ♗b5** *(1a)*. This looks less scary than 3 ♗c4 as White doesn't target the f7-pawn, but White's plan is to put pressure on the e5-pawn by attacking its defender. Sooner or later, Black will need to parry this threat, and White hopes to use the time gained to establish a strong grip on the centre. Note also that Black's pawn-thrust ...d5, which we saw repeatedly in the Giuoco Piano and Two Knights, will not hit the bishop. Black has a wide choice of replies, as White isn't yet threatening 4 ♗xc6 dxc6 5 ♘xe5, because 5...♕d4 regains the pawn with a good game. Thus 3...d6 is unnecessarily passive, and 4 d4 gives White the freer game. The main line is 3...a6, with points like 4 ♗a4 d6 5 d4?! b5! 6 ♗b3 ♘xd4 7 ♘xd4 exd4 8 ♕xd4?? c5, when ...c4 will win the white bishop. The solid 3...♘f6 *(3)* and the wild 3...f5 *(4)* are also possible, while the natural 3...♗c5 leaves the bishop exposed to White's c3 and d4 pawn-break.

Basic Positions of the Ruy Lopez

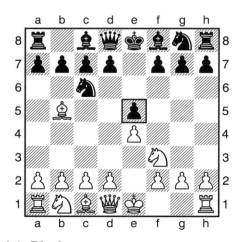

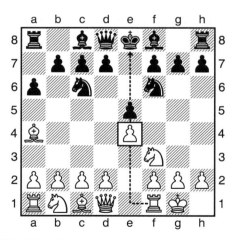

1a) Black moves

3...a6 forces the bishop to declare its intentions. For 4 ♗xc6 dxc6 see diagram 2a. 4 ♗a4 keeps the bishop, waiting for a better moment to exchange on c6.

1b) Black moves

Then 4...♘f6 5 0-0 leads to this position. It looks as if White has forgotten about his e-pawn, but see page 40 for 5...♘xe4. The main move is 5...♗e7 (pages 36-9).

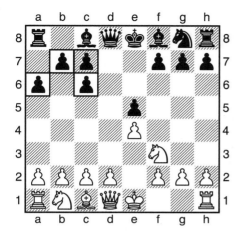

2a) White moves

After 5 d4 exd4 6 ♕xd4 ♕xd4 7 ♘xd4, a pure pawn ending would be bad for Black, so he must avoid too many exchanges and put his strong bishops to work. 5 ♘xe5 ♕d4 gives White nothing.

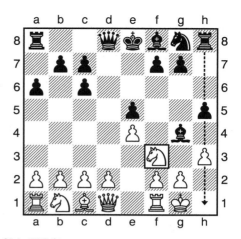

2b) White moves

The position after 5 0-0 ♗g4!? 6 h3 h5!. The bishop is taboo: 7 hxg4? hxg4 8 ♘h2? ♕h4. After 7 d3 ♕f6 Black intends ...♘e7-g6 and may exchange on f3 if this doubles White's pawns too.

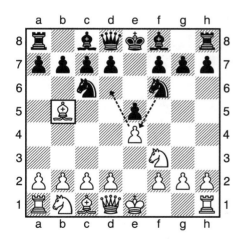

3) White moves

This defence has the idea 4 0-0 ♘xe4 5 ♖e1 ♘d6, attacking the b5-bishop. This pops up again in the line 5 d4 ♘d6 6 ♗xc6 dxc6 7 dxe5 ♘f5 8 ♕xd8+ ♔xd8, with a complex queenless middlegame.

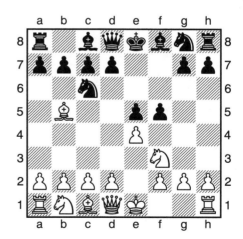

4) White moves

A point of this thrust is 4 d4 fxe4 5 ♘xe5 ♘xe5 6 dxe5 c6. If the bishop moves, 7...♕a5+ wins the e5-pawn. After 4 ♘c3 fxe4 5 ♘xe4 ♘f6 6 ♘xf6+ ♕xf6 7 ♕e2 ♗e7 Black offers a pawn to get piece-play.

35

A true test of chess understanding

1 e4 e5 2 ♘f3 ♘c6 3 ♗b5 a6 4 ♗a4 ♘f6 5 0-0 ♗e7 *(1a)* is known as the Closed Ruy Lopez, and often leads to play of great strategic subtlety. But don't be fooled by the name: there are plenty of ways for the game to open up. First things first though: White now needs to protect his e4-pawn, so 6 ♖e1 is the normal move. White then threatens to exchange on c6 and take on e5, so Black prevents this idea with 6...b5 7 ♗b3. You might think that White has simply lost time with this bishop, but it has arrived on a very good diagonal, and Black's moves ...a6 and ...b5 can provide useful targets for White. Having secured his e5-pawn, Black needs to decide how to deploy his pieces. 7...d6 is the standard move, bringing in ideas of ...♗g4 and also with the positional threat of ...♘a5, exchanging off White's potent bishop. That's why White normally replies 8 c3 *(1b)*, which also prepares the move d4. Then after 8...0-0 9 h3 *(2a)* we have reached a position where Black has a very wide choice of plans.

Basic Positions of the Closed Ruy Lopez

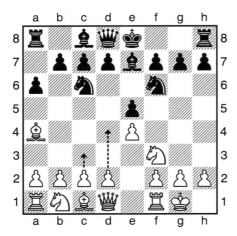

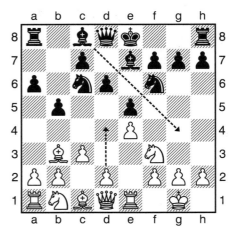

1a) White moves

Direct attacking methods achieve little for White here. His best plan is to secure his e-pawn and play c3 and d4, building a strong and flexible pawn-centre.

1b) Black moves

Now 8...♘a5 gets nowhere after 9 ♗c2. Following 8...0-0 9 d4, Black's 9...♗g4! idea puts pressure on White, as 10 h3? ♗xf3 11 ♕xf3 exd4 costs him a pawn.

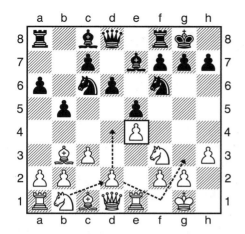

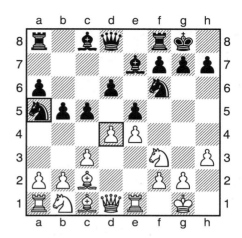

2a) Black moves

White plans d4, with an ideal centre, and then to develop by ♘bd2, and if possible ♘f1-g3, freeing the c1-bishop. Black's main defences all hinder this manoeuvre – see the next three diagrams.

2b) Black moves

This is the Chigorin Defence, 9...♘a5 10 ♗c2 c5 11 d4. Now 11...♕c7 12 ♘bd2 ♘c6 13 d5 closes the game, 11...cxd4 12 cxd4 exd4 opens it, while 11...♘d7 12 ♘bd2 exd4 13 cxd4 unbalances matters.

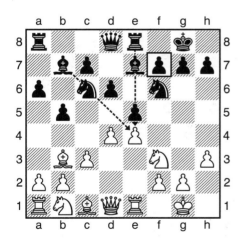

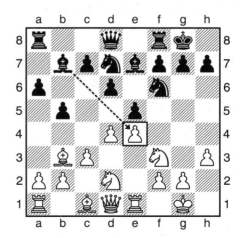

2c) White moves

9...♗b7 10 d4 ♖e8 puts direct pressure on e4, and can lead to exciting play in lines like 11 ♘bd2 ♗f8 12 a4 h6 13 ♗c2 exd4 14 cxd4 ♘b4 15 ♗b1 c5. But note 11 ♘g5 ♖f8 12 ♘f3, seeking a draw.

2d) White moves

Breyer's 9...♘b8 10 d4 ♘bd7 11 ♘bd2 ♗b7 reorganizes Black's pieces flexibly, with ...d5 and ...c5 both still possible. The two players must manoeuvre carefully, ready for many different structures.

A sensational but subtle gambit

The Marshall Attack is a daring gambit by Black. Just as White is settling down to put his opponent under long-term pressure, Black gives away a central pawn, blasting open lines and targeting the white king. But unlike many other gambits, this one is often played by the world's best grandmasters. After **1 e4 e5 2 ♘f3 ♘c6 3 ♗b5 a6 4 ♗a4 ♘f6 5 0-0 ♗e7 6 ♖e1 b5 7 ♗b3**, Black must choose **7...0-0** if he wishes to play the Marshall. That's because the idea is to meet **8 c3** with **8...d5** *(1a)* (and not 8...d6, returning to the Closed lines). After 9 exd5 ♘xd5 (for 9...e4?! 10 dxc6 exf3 see diagram 4) 10 ♘xe5 ♘xe5 11 ♖xe5 c6 *(1b)*, Black plans ...♗d6 and a rapid deployment of his pieces towards White's kingside, gaining time attacking the white rook. The now slow-looking move c3 means that White's queenside will sleep for some time to come. The battle will revolve around White's attempts to parry the kingside threats without making too many positional concessions. We also look at 8 a4 *(5)*, White's principal 'Anti-Marshall' move.

Basic Positions of the Marshall Attack

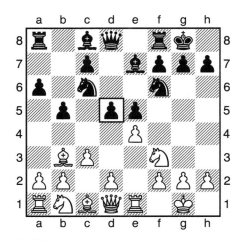

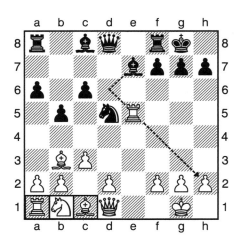

1a) White moves
Black loses the e5-pawn, but is left with very active pieces. The light squares around the white king can prove weak, with their main defender far away on b3.

1b) White moves
Black's ideas include ...♗d6 and ...♕h4, followed by ...♗g4 and ...♖ae8-e6-h6 or the pawn-storm ...f5-f4. Can White even survive? See the next two diagrams!

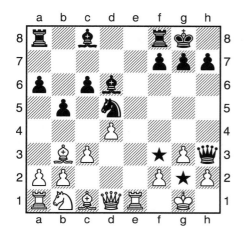

2) White moves

This is after 12 d4 &d6 13 &e1 &h4 14 g3 &h3. One idea is 15 &e4 g5! 16 &f1 &h5, but 15 &e3 &g4 16 &d3 &ae8 17 &d2 &e6 is more common. Either way, White remains under pressure.

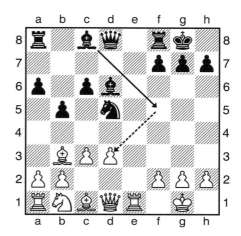

3) Black moves

White has chosen 12 d3 &d6 13 &e1. With the rook defended, 13...&h4 14 g3 &h3 15 &e4 g5? allows 16 &xg5. But White's play is slow, and after the calm 13...&f5, White finds it hard to unravel.

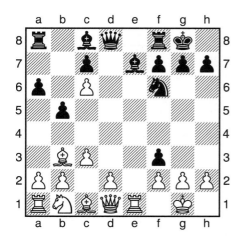

4) White moves

White is better here, but his king is under fire after both 11 &xf3 &g4 12 &g3 &e8 13 f3 &d3! and 11 d4 fxg2 12 &f3 a5 intending ...a4, ...b4 and ...&a5. 11 g3!? &g4 12 d4 keeps more control.

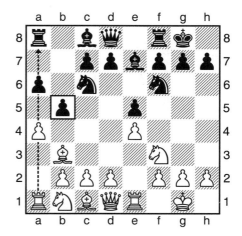

5) Black moves

Thanks to Black avoiding ...d6, White threatens axb5 at a time when ...&g4 is impossible and ...&a5 drops the e5-pawn. But 8...b4 9 d3 d6 10 a5 &b8 is OK – whose advanced pawn is weaker?

It's all about active pieces

Like the Marshall Attack, the Open Spanish is a way for Black to smash open the centre and develop his pieces actively. In this case though, Black doesn't sacrifice a pawn, and White also gets a healthy portion of the fun. A middlegame of intricate cut-and-thrust tactics often follows. After **1 e4 e5 2 ♘f3 ♘c6 3 ♗b5 a6 4 ♗a4 ♘f6 5 0-0**, Black plays **5...♘xe4** *(1a)*. In earlier sections, we noted that this pawn is often too hot for Black to grab, but he has a specific idea in mind here. After 6 d4! (opening lines; 6 ♖e1 ♘c5 works out fine for Black), he plays 6...b5 7 ♗b3 d5 (not 7...exd4? 8 ♖e1 d5 9 ♘c3!!) 8 dxe5 ♗e6 *(1b)*. Black has returned the pawn, freed his pieces and secured a foothold in the centre. On the other hand, his position is a little loose, and White may be able to gain time with threats against the e4-knight. Black must scramble to complete his development without suffering any accidents, but structurally, a key idea is for Black to unify his pawns with a later ...c5. We also look at 6...exd4 7 ♖e1 d5 *(4)*, the Riga Variation.

Basic Positions of the Open Spanish

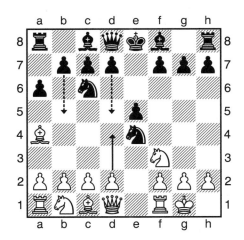

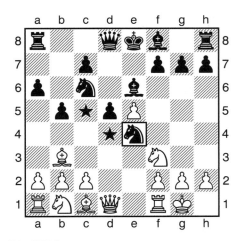

1a) White moves

6 d4! robs the black knight of the c5-square and seeks to open the e-file. Due to 6...d5? 7 ♘xe5 ♗d7 8 ♘xf7! ♔xf7 9 ♕h5+, Black needs to play 6...b5 before ...d5.

1b) White moves

Look at Black's active pieces! But if White gets a firm grip over d4, he will be better. He can start with 9 c3 ♗c5 *(3)* or 9 ♘bd2 *(2a)*, targeting the black knight.

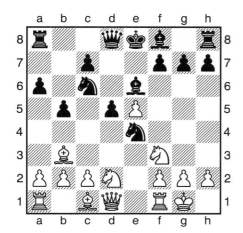

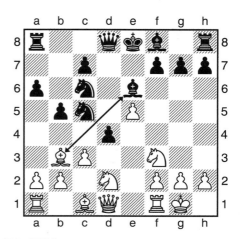

2a) Black moves

The e4-knight is feeling the heat already, with lines like 9...♗c5?! 10 ♘xe4 dxe4 11 ♘g5 not to Black's liking. 9...♗e7 10 c3 0-0 11 ♖e1 gives White pressure. 9...♘c5 10 c3 d4 (*2b*) is more ambitious.

2b) White moves

Now 11 ♗xe6 ♘xe6 12 cxd4 ♘cxd4 13 a4 is the positional approach, while 11 ♘g5!? is a sensational idea, based on 11...♕xg5 12 ♕f3!, when Black has no good way to keep his extra piece.

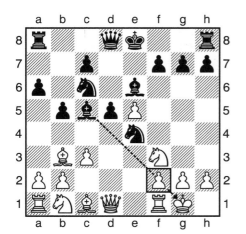

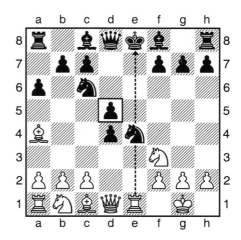

3) White moves

An example of Black's piece-play is 10 ♘bd2 0-0 11 ♗c2 ♘xf2 12 ♖xf2 f6, with great complications. 10 ♕d3 prepares ♘bd2, but 10...♘e7 11 ♘bd2 ♗f5 firmly supports the e4-knight.

4) White moves

8 ♘xd4 looks devastating, but the idea is 8...♗d6 9 ♘xc6 ♗xh2+!, with a draw if White takes on h2. 8 c4!? is an ambitious gambit: 8...♗b4 9 cxd5 or 8...dxc3 9 ♘xc3 ♗e6 (9...♗b4 10 ♘xe4) 10 ♘e5.

Alekhine Defence

Cunning provocation – or foolish impudence?

The Alekhine Defence is one of the most aggressive and provocative replies to **1 e4**.
With **1...♞f6** *(1a)*, Black threatens the white pawn, challenging it to advance and chase
the black knight. If it does so, Black will round on the impudent white pawn, and keep
attacking any of White's pieces and pawns that come to its aid. While ambitious, the
Alekhine is also a risky defence, as the early confrontation can leave Black's position
disorganized and short of space. The most critical lines begin after 2 e5 ♞d5 3 d4 d6.
The main line is the solid and flexible 4 ♞f3, while the Four Pawns Attack is an attempt
to smash Black flat with 4 c4 ♞b6 5 f4 dxe5 6 fxe5 *(2a)*. This leads to chaotic positions
where it looks as if the pieces have been dropped randomly onto the board! Another popular system is 4 c4 ♞b6 5 exd6 *(3)*, the sedate Exchange Variation, while the Chase Variation, 3 c4 ♞b6 4 c5 ♞d5 *(4)*, is like chess from another planet!

Basic Positions of the Alekhine Defence

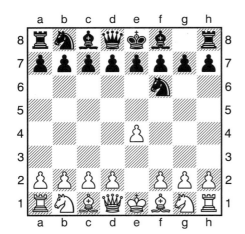

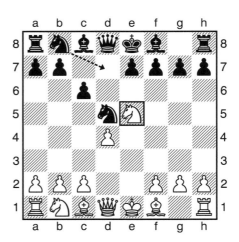

1a) White moves
After 2 e5 ♞d5 3 d4 d6 4 ♞f3, Black's traditional reply is 4...♝g4, but after 5 ♝e2
it can be hard to challenge White's space
advantage. Modern grandmasters prefer
the solid 4...dxe5 5 ♞xe5 c6 *(1b)*.

1b) White moves
This little pawn move prepares ...♞d7
(not 5...♞d7?! 6 ♞xf7! with an attack)
and keeps options of a set-up with either
...g6 or ...e6. Note that after 6 c4 ♞b4!,
Black threatens 7...♛xd4 8 ♛xd4 ♞c2+.

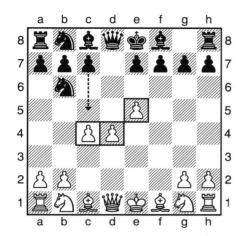

2a) Black moves

One sharp way to attack the centre is 6...c5 7 d5 g6 8 ♘c3 ♗g7 9 ♗f4 0-0 10 ♕d2 e6, but the main line goes 6...♘c6 7 ♗e3 ♗f5 8 ♘c3 e6 9 ♘f3 ♗e7 *(2b)*.

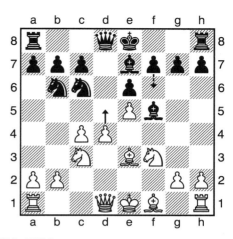

2b) White moves

Soon ...f6 will break up White's centre, so White strikes first by 10 d5 exd5 11 cxd5 ♘b4 12 ♘d4 ♗d7. Then 13 ♕f3 is calm, and 13 e6 crazily complex!

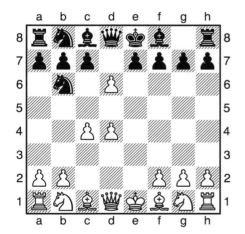

3) Black moves

White has a small space advantage and hopes the knight will be misplaced on b6, despite its attack upon c4. 5...cxd6 6 ♘c3 g6 7 ♗e3 ♗g7 8 ♖c1 0-0 9 b3 e5 is a popular line where White bolsters this pawn and Black hits back in the centre.

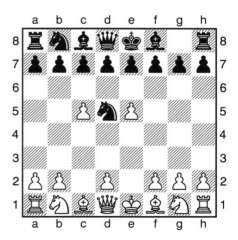

4) White moves

Anything is possible here; 5 ♗c4 c6 6 ♘c3 d6 7 ♕b3 ♘d7 8 ♘xd5 ♘xc5 9 ♘c7+ ♔d7 is typical cut-and-thrust play if White just attacks the knight. But Black should avoid 5 ♗c4 e6 6 ♘c3 d6?! 7 ♘xd5 exd5 8 ♗xd5 c6 9 ♗xf7+! with three pawns for a piece.

Simplicity – but at what cost?

If you are looking for a simple, easy-to-learn answer to **1 e4** that gives White very little choice, then **1...d5** *(1a)* is ideal. The only testing reply is 2 exd5, but any hopes White had of a blocked position or creating a big pawn-centre are gone. Black can regain the pawn in two ways, and look forward to developing his pieces freely.

Of course, it isn't quite as simple as that. White also has very free development, and Black will need to spend some time recapturing his pawn. After the straightforward 2...♕xd5 3 ♘c3, we already see that Black must lose more time with his queen, and we saw an example in the Introduction to this book how perilous that can be. But with care (normally that means playing ...c6 quite soon!), Black can gain an acceptable position after either 3...♕a5 4 d4 *(1b)* or the more modern 3...♕d6 4 d4 ♘f6 5 ♘f3 *(2)*. Black's other option, 2...♘f6, is more ambitious. We shall take a look at the obvious 3 c4 *(3)* and the exciting 3 d4 ♗g4!? *(4)*, and note that the modest 3 ♘f3 *(5)* may be best.

Basic Positions of the Scandinavian Defence

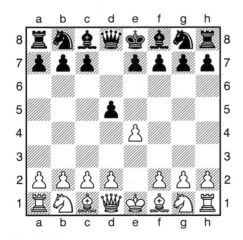

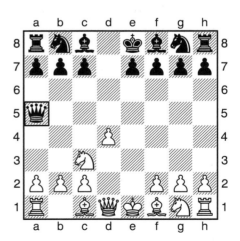

1a) White moves

White has little choice but to exchange on d5. Otherwise Black has 'got away with' playing the highly desirable move ...d5 without preparing it by ...e6 or ...c6.

1b) Black moves

4...♘f6 5 ♘f3 c6 6 ♗c4 ♗f5 is a typical continuation. One plan is ...e6, ...♗b4 and ...♗xc3, giving up the bishop-pair but gaining a firm grip on the d5-square.

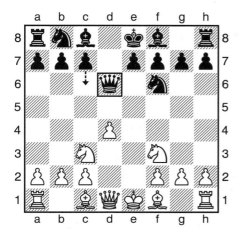

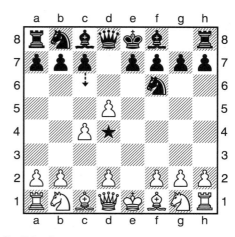

2) Black moves

A popular position. 5...g6 6 ②b5 ♕b6 7 c4 c6, 5...c6 6 ②e5 ②bd7 7 ②c4 ♕c7 and 5...a6 (keeping ...②c6 ideas open) 6 g3 ♗g4 7 ♗g2 c6!? all see Black manoeuvring carefully to avoid 'accidents'.

3) Black moves

Has Black lost a pawn for nothing? No: 3...c6! is an excellent gambit. 4 dxc6?! ②xc6 gives Black a superb grip on d4 and the centre, and leaves White's pawns weak. 4 d4 cxd5 is covered on page 47.

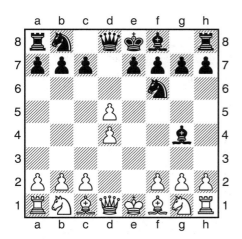

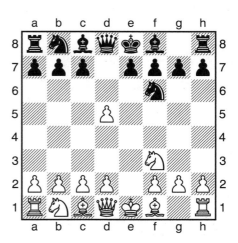

4) White moves

This is a neat idea for Black. 4 ②f3 ♕xd5 gives Black additional ideas with ...♕h5, while 4 f3 ♗f5 5 c4 e6! 6 dxe6 ②c6! leads to crazy gambit play. After 7 exf7+? ♔xf7, Black attacks on the e-file.

5) Black moves

3...♗g4?! 4 ♗b5+ is awkward for Black, while 3...♕xd5 4 ②c3 is similar to the 2...♕xd5 lines. 3...②xd5 4 d4, with c4 often to follow soon, gives White a space advantage. Black must tread carefully.

Caro-Kann Defence

Extreme solidity – but many sharp options for both players

This oddly-named opening features the equally odd little move **1...c6** *(1a)* in answer to **1 e4**. Yet it is one of the most respectable and popular openings, appealing to both club players and grandmasters. Black's idea is to play 2...d5. Compared to the French Defence (page 48), Black has not blocked in his queen's bishop. Compared to the Scandinavian, Black can recapture on d5 with a pawn. Those are the good points – the dark side is that ...c6 is a slow move that doesn't prepare to develop a piece.

After 2 d4 d5, White's e-pawn is under attack, so what should he do? The Panov Attack, 3 exd5 cxd5 4 c4 *(4)*, opens the game and often gives White active piece-play and an isolated queen's pawn. 3 e5 is the aggressive Advance Variation, when after the logical 3...♗f5 *(5)*, White has ideas of hunting down this active but exposed bishop. The main lines start after 3 ♘c3 (or 3 ♘d2), when Black has nothing better than 3...dxe4 4 ♘xe4 *(1b)*. White is a little freer, but Black can develop easily.

Basic Positions of the Caro-Kann Defence

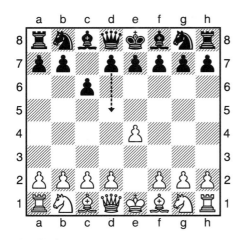

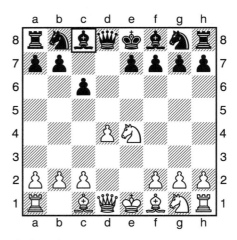

1a) White moves

Black intends ...d5, contesting White's central foothold. The plan will then be to place his queen's bishop actively on f5 or g4 and develop his pieces rapidly.

1b) Black moves

The main ideas here are 4...♗f5 5 ♘g3 ♗g6 *(2)*, which develops the bishop but also lets White pursue it, and 4...♘d7 *(3)*, blocking the bishop but planning 5...♘gf6.

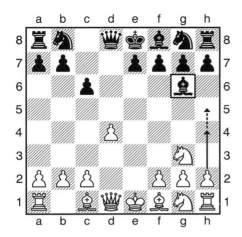

2) White moves

Simple development gives White little, so 6 h4 h6 7 ♘f3 ♘d7 8 h5 ♗h7 9 ♗d3 ♗xd3 10 ♕xd3 is normal. White has staked out space, and has the makings of a kingside attack, if Black castles there.

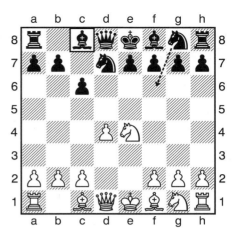

3) White moves

Now 5 ♕e2?! threatens instant mate, but 5...♘df6! neatly parries. 5 ♘g5!? ♘gf6 (5...h6?! 6 ♘e6!) 6 ♗d3 e6 7 ♘1f3 has the cunning idea 7...h6?! 8 ♘xe6! fxe6 9 ♗g6+ ♔e7 10 0-0, with a strong attack.

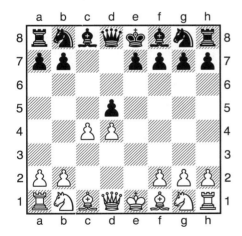

4) Black moves

This looks like a Queen's Gambit, but after 4...♘f6 5 ♘c3, odd lines like 5...g6 6 ♕b3 ♗g7 and 5...♘c6 6 ♗g5 ♗e6 are possible. 5...e6 6 ♘f3 ♗e7 7 cxd5 ♘xd5 leads to typical 'isolated-pawn' play.

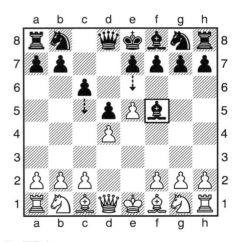

5) White moves

Primitive play like 4 g4?! ♗e4 5 f3 ♗g6 6 h4 h5 gives White nothing, but 4 ♘c3 prepares g4 with much greater effect. White can also play more quietly, with 4 ♗e3 a flexible way to keep options open.

47

French Defence: Introduction

Deceptively provocative

The French Defence begins **1 e4 e6** *(1a)*, almost always followed by 2 d4 d5. It is a weapon for counterattackers. After 2...d5, White has several ways to respond to the threat of 3...dxe4. The Advance Variation, 3 e5, cramps Black's pieces, when 3...c5 4 c3 ♘c6 5 ♘f3 gives us Diagram 1b. White's 'pawn-chain' (pawns on c3, d4 and e5) appears in most lines of the French (an exception is the Exchange Variation, 3 exd5 exd5, which is too simplistic and symmetrical to give Black real problems). In the main line, Black attacks and White defends d4: 5...♕b6 6 ♗e2 cxd4 7 cxd4 ♘h6 8 b3 ♘f5 9 ♗b2 *(2)*. 3 ♘d2 is the Tarrasch Variation. After 3...c5 4 exd5 exd5 5 ♘gf3 ♘c6 6 ♗b5 *(3)*, isolated pawn positions arise. 3...♘f6 provokes 4 e5 ♘fd7, when 5 ♗d3 c5 6 c3 ♘c6 establishes the familiar pawn-chain. After 7 ♘e2, 7...cxd4 8 cxd4 f6 9 exf6 ♘xf6 10 ♘f3 ♗d6 *(4)* is normal, while 7 ♘gf3 might provoke Black to attack by 7...♗e7 8 0-0 g5!? *(5)*.

Basic Positions of the French Defence

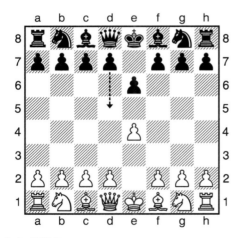

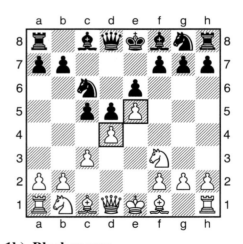

1a) White moves

White normally grabs more of the centre with 2 d4, and Black challenges on the light squares by playing 2...d5. A principled response is 3 e5, trying to stifle Black's pieces. For 3 ♘c3 see page 50.

1b) Black moves

To free his pieces from White's grip, Black will have to capture or trade off the pawns on d4 and e5. If White can maintain them, especially the one on e5, he will have the advantage in space and mobility.

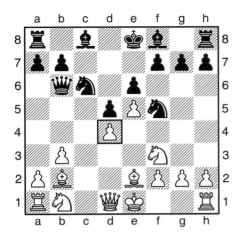

2) Black moves

Black has maximized his attack on d4 and White his defence. Now 9...♗b4+! forces 10 ♔f1, or else Black captures the d-pawn. But White still has his extra space, so both sides have chances.

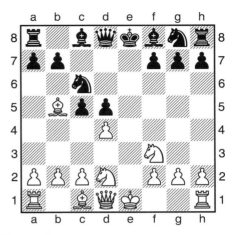

3) Black moves

White's pawn-centre vanishes after 6...♗d6 7 dxc5 ♗xc5 8 0-0 ♘e7. Black has good activity, but fewer pieces out, and his isolated pawn can become a target later in the game as more pieces are exchanged.

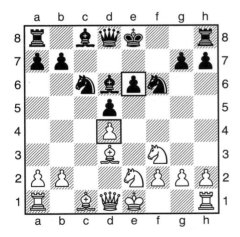

4) White moves

Black has a backward and vulnerable pawn on e6, and White's pawn on d4 is isolated. White would like to exchange Black's good bishop on d6 by ♗f4, while Black hopes for ...e5 or play on the f-file.

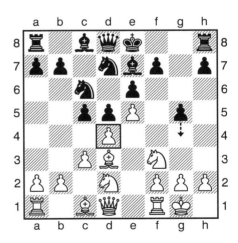

5) White moves

Black is using a caveman-style attack to drive White's knight away from f3 and win the d4-pawn. The drawback is that this might simply leave Black's own kingside weak. A challenging fight lies ahead.

Going for the maximum

After **1 e4 e6 2 d4 d5, 3 ♘c3** *(1a)* is the most popular move, since it protects e4, attacks d5, develops a piece, and keeps paths open for both bishops. Black's natural reply 3...♘f6 provokes White to advance by 4 e5, when 4...♘fd7 5 f4 c5 6 ♘f3 ♘c6 7 ♗e3 *(1b)* battles for d4. A famous gambit goes 3...♘f6 4 ♗g5 ♗e7 5 e5 ♘fd7 6 h4!?, sacrificing a pawn with the idea 6...♗xg5 7 hxg5 ♕xg5 8 ♘h3 *(2)*. Black can also play 4...♗b4, the MacCutcheon Variation, which usually continues 5 e5 h6 6 ♗d2 ♗xc3 7 bxc3 ♘e4 8 ♕g4 *(3)*. The Winawer Variation is 3...♗b4, threatening ...dxe4. The main line goes 4 e5 c5 5 a3 ♗xc3+ 6 bxc3 ♘e7 *(4)*. Now White's sharpest move is 7 ♕g4, attacking g7, and Black's most ambitious response is 7...♕c7 8 ♕xg7 ♖g8 9 ♕xh7 cxd4 *(5)*, the Winawer Poisoned Pawn variation. Black temporarily sacrifices a pawn so he can attack on the queenside. Players have slugged it out in this position for many years.

Basic Positions of the 3 ♘c3 French Defence

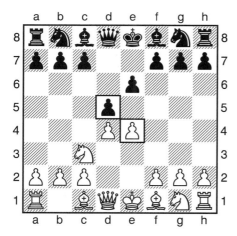

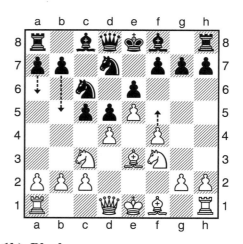

1a) Black moves

3 ♘c3 is White's most logical move. It develops a piece (unlike 3 e5) and keeps open lines for both bishops (unlike 3 ♘d2). A traditional answer is 3...♘f6. 3...dxe4 is simpler, but less active.

1b) Black moves

White has bolstered his centre. He typically develops by ♗e2 and 0-0, hoping for a kingside attack with f5. Black has extra territory on the queenside and can prepare an advance with ...a6 and ...b5.

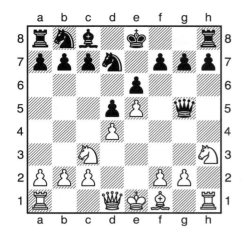

2) Black moves

Why has White sacrificed a pawn? For faster development, space and play on the h-file. ♘f4, ♕g4 and 0-0-0 can follow quickly. Of course, Black has an extra pawn and no structural weaknesses.

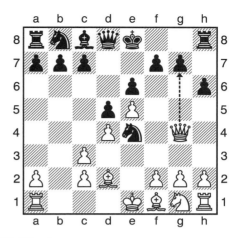

3) Black moves

Now 8...0-0? allows 9 ♗xh6!, so 8...g6 9 ♗d3 ♘xd2 10 ♔xd2 c5 is normal. Then White can attack Black's kingside, but White's king is stuck in the centre. A sharp game results.

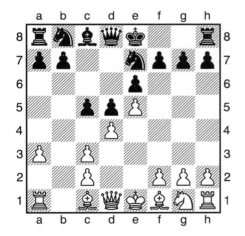

4) White moves

White has the bishop-pair and he controls more space on the kingside thanks to the e5-pawn. However, his doubled c-pawns are weak and Black has fast development with active play on the queenside.

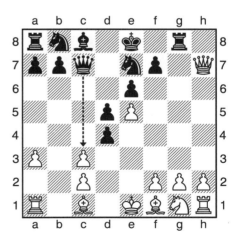

5) White moves

Black's kingside is destroyed, but he has the safer king, rapid development and very active pieces. Here 10 ♘e2! defends c3 and attacks d4. In response, 10...♘bc6! sets the trap 11 cxd4? ♘xd4!.

Sound, flexible and aggressive

The Sicilian is the most popular opening at club level, and all the way up to world-championship chess. But what is it about **1 e4 c5** *(1a)* that appeals so much?

Firstly, Black prevents White from setting up an 'ideal' centre with pawns on e4 and d4. If White plays d4, then Black will exchange by ...cxd4, when he will have more centre pawns than White, a strategic plus that strong players are willing to suffer for. And suffer Black may, as White is well-placed to start an attack in almost any sector of the board. But Black has many sources of counterplay: pressure on the half-open c-file, tactics on the long h8-a1 diagonal, and well-timed pawn-thrusts. Many years of testing have shown that the Sicilian is fundamentally sound for Black and, critically, that he can play for a win without taking extreme risks. White has no easy way to seek a risk-free edge; this is an opening of boat-burning risk-taking, where the brave (and knowledgeable!) prevail.

Basic Positions of the Sicilian Defence

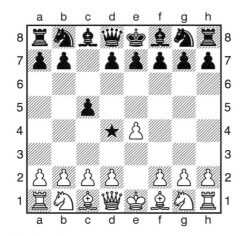

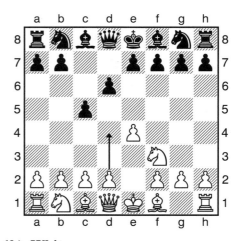

1a) White moves
The main battleground is the 'Open Sicilian', where White plays 2 ♘f3 and 3 d4. But there are many other possibilities, such as 2 c3 intending d4, and 2 ♘c3 followed by either f4 or g3.

1b) White moves
The situation after 2 ♘f3 d6. Now 3 d4 cxd4 4 ♘xd4 ♘f6 5 ♘c3 is the main system (pages 62-7), but 3 ♗b5+ is also popular (page 60). 3 c3 can be met by 3...♘f6, when 4 d4? drops the e4-pawn.

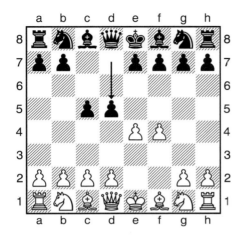

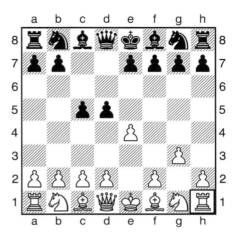

2) White moves

Black has answered 2 f4 with 2...d5!. The
...d5 advance is an important idea in many
Sicilian lines – so White normally prevents it! The gambit 3 exd5 ♘f6! 4 c4 e6 5
dxe6 ♗xe6 gives Black good play.

3) White moves

2 g3 d5 is another line where White has
failed to control this key square. After 3
exd5 ♕xd5 4 ♘f3 ♗g4 5 ♗g2 ♕e6+,
White's position lacks punch: he must exchange queens or misplace his king.

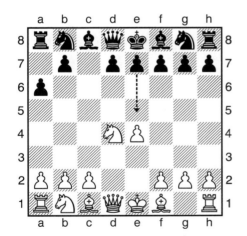

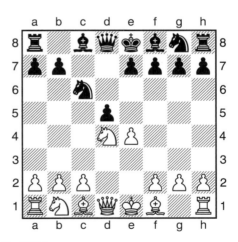

4) Black moves

2 ♘f3 a6 3 d4?! cxd4 4 ♘xd4 is a surpris-
ing case of careless play (3 c3 is better).
By 4...♘f6 5 ♘c3 (5 e5? ♕a5+) 5...e5! 6
♘b3 ♗b4 7 ♗d3 d5!, Black activates his
pieces and seizes the initiative.

5) White moves

But this position, from 2 ♘f3 ♘c6 3 d4
cxd4 4 ♘xd4 d5?!, is another story. After
5 ♗b5 dxe4 6 ♘xc6 ♕xd1+ 7 ♔xd1 a6 8
♗a4 ♗d7 9 ♘c3 ♗xc6 10 ♗xc6+ bxc6 11
♘xe4 Black has a difficult endgame.

Controlled aggression

White's most aggressive plan against the Sicilian is to play d4 and use his lead in development to launch an attack. But he can also develop more cautiously, clamping down on Black's ...d5 advance. The Closed Sicilian starts with **1 e4 c5 2 ♘c3**. After the standard (but not forced!) reply **2...♘c6**, White needs to play purposefully; otherwise Black can soon advance in the centre or on the queenside, and make good use of his grip on the d4-square. White normally advances his f-pawn, seizing space and starting a kingside attack. He can do so immediately by **3 f4** *(1b)* or first choose **3 g3** *(1a)* and 4 ♗g2, exerting pressure on the long diagonal. Typically, neither player will develop his king's knight in front of his f-pawn. Even though both players are seeking to attack on the wing (White on the kingside and Black on the queenside), central control is vital for the success of these plans. Black must also remember that 3 ♘f3 *(5)*, intending 4 d4, is possible.

Basic Positions of the Closed Sicilian and Grand Prix Attack

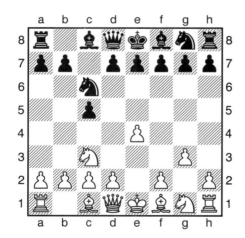

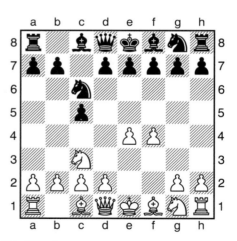

1a) Black moves

White plans a gradual build-up on the kingside, although he can also play in the centre with d4 or on the queenside by ♖b1, a3 and b4. After 3...g6 4 ♗g2 ♗g7 5 d3 d6 *(4)* some subtle play is needed.

1b) Black moves

The Grand Prix Attack. It is most dangerous when Black plays an early ...d6. Compare 3...g6 4 ♘f3 ♗g7 5 ♗c4 e6 *(2)* with 3...d6 4 ♘f3 g6 5 ♗c4 (5 ♗b5 is good too) 5...♗g7 6 0-0 ♘f6 7 d3 *(3)*.

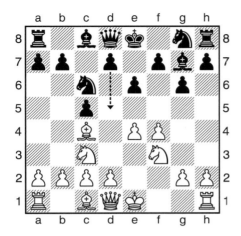

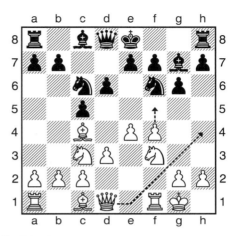

2) White moves

Black plans the central strike ...♘ge7 and ...d5, scattering the white pieces. Even the gambit 6 f5 does not prevent 6...♘ge7! 7 fxe6 fxe6 8 d3 d5 9 ♗b3 b5!, when White can easily lose a piece.

3) Black moves

Mating ideas with ♕h4, ♗h6 and ♘g5 are crude but powerful, and an e5 thrust can also come into play. In lines like 7...0-0 8 f5!? gxf5 9 ♕e1 fxe4 10 dxe4 ♗g4 11 ♕h4 Black must be very careful.

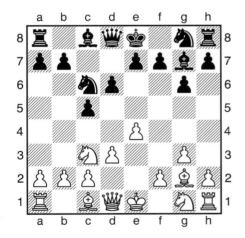

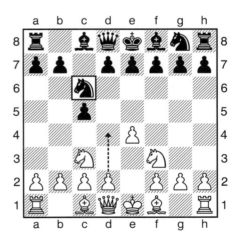

4) White moves

6 ♗e3 plans ♕d2 and ♗h6, so 6...e5 makes sense, keeping Black's other bishop active. 6 f4 seeks to smother Black on the kingside. The flexible 6...e6 and ...♘ge7 guards the key f5-square.

5) Black moves

White plans 4 d4 with an Open Sicilian. If Black wanted to play a Najdorf (page 66), he should have chosen 2...d6 last move! But Dragon players (page 64) can be happy after 3...g6 4 d4 cxd4 5 ♘xd4 ♗g7.

Alapin (c3) Sicilian

Simply building a pawn-centre

This is one of the most popular ways for White to meet the Sicilian, as it keeps the game fairly simple while still being ambitious and logical. After **1 e4 c5**, White plays **2 c3** *(1a)*, preparing to play d4, when he will be ready to recapture with the c3-pawn if Black exchanges pawns on d4. This would give White an 'ideal' pawn-centre, with unopposed pawns on e4 and d4, without making any weaknesses or losing time. If Black had to accept that situation, then the Sicilian wouldn't be a very popular opening at all! In fact, Black has two very reliable replies, both based on the fact that the move c3 is a little clumsy, and both playing by analogy with other openings that we have seen earlier.

2...♘f6 is similar to an Alekhine Defence, but after 3 e5 ♘d5 *(3)*, the natural 4 c4 would be a loss of time (White has taken two moves to play his pawn to c4). 2...d5 3 exd5 ♕xd5 4 d4 *(1b)* is like a Scandinavian where White cannot play ♘c3 right now, and this means the queen is more secure in the centre. But ideas of dxc5 or ♘a3-b5 are in the air.

Basic Positions of the Alapin (c3) Sicilian

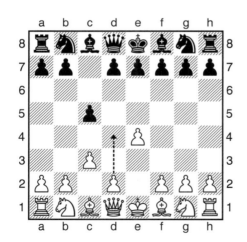

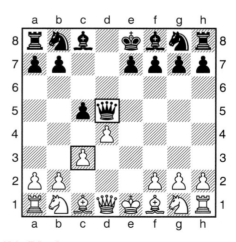

1a) Black moves

There is a wide choice, with 2...e6 3 d4 d5 similar to a French, and 2...e5 3 ♘f3 ♘c6 4 ♗c4 ♕c7 an odd form of Italian Game. But targeting e4 is more logical.

1b) Black moves

If Black exchanges on d4 too fast, ♘c3 will gain time on the queen, and White might launch a vicious attack. 4...♘f6 5 ♘f3 ♗g4 *(2)* develops actively.

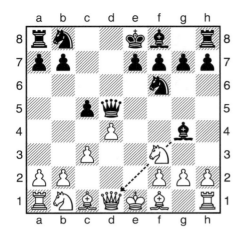

2) White moves

6 ♗e2 e6 7 0-0 ♘c6 8 ♗e3 cxd4 9 cxd4 ♗e7 10 ♘c3 ♕d6 leaves Black comfortable, and 6 ♕a4+ ♗d7 7 ♕b3 cxd4! 8 ♗c4 ♕e4+ is a wild ride. 6 dxc5!? keeps control, proposing a complex ending.

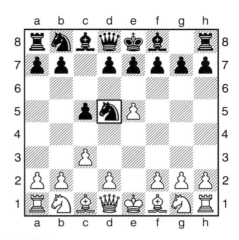

3) White moves

The plan for White is to advance in the centre while putting pressure on the d5-knight. He can do so by the obvious 4 d4 cxd4 *(4)* or 4 ♘f3 ♘c6 5 ♗c4 ♘b6 6 ♗b3 *(5)*, with d4 possibly coming later.

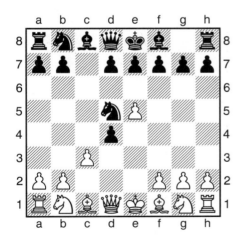

4) White moves

5 cxd4 d6 successfully attacks the white pawns. 5 ♘f3 is more cunning, but 5...♘c6 6 ♗c4 ♘b6 7 ♗b3 d5! 8 exd6 ♕xd6 9 0-0 ♗e6! is a vigorous sequence that neutralizes White's powerful bishop.

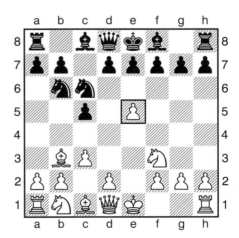

5) Black moves

After 6...d5 7 exd6 ♕xd6 8 ♘a3! we see White finding a more useful move than d4. 6...c4 7 ♗c2 ♕c7 is ambitious, as d4 is still met by ...cxd3, and 8 ♕e2 g5! offers to exchange g-pawn for e-pawn.

Morra Gambit

A great way to get Sicilian players on the run

The Morra Gambit is an aggressive reply to the Sicilian. **1 e4 c5 2 d4 cxd4 3 c3** *(1a)* sur-
renders a pawn, but if Black accepts it, he must find his way through a minefield of tactics and traps. After 3...dxc3 4 ♘xc3 ♘c6 5 ♘f3, White has a development advantage,
and ideas of playing e5 make it hard for Black to catch up. In many lines, White's next
moves will be ♗c4, 0-0, ♕e2 and ♖d1, creating several threats and giving the black
queen problems finding a good square. Diagram 2a features the position after 5...d6 6
♗c4 e6 7 0-0 a6 8 ♕e2 ♘f6 9 ♖d1 ♕c7 10 ♗f4, where Black has played very normal Sicilian moves but is in danger. If Black prefers to be the one setting traps, he can try the
Siberian Trap: 5...e6 6 ♗c4 ♕c7 7 0-0 ♘f6 *(3)*, when it is easy for White to lose in just
two more moves! But this line also has its risks for Black. The Chicago Defence features
the imaginative rook manoeuvre 5...d6 6 ♗c4 a6 7 0-0 e6 8 ♕e2 b5 9 ♗b3 ♖a7 *(4)*.

Basic Positions of the Morra Gambit

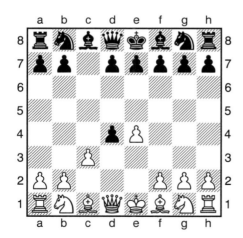

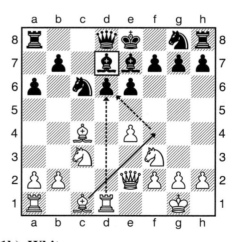

1a) Black moves

3...♘f6 4 e5 ♘d5 safely declines the pawn
(see page 57). After 3...dxc3 4 ♘xc3 ♘c6 5
♘f3, one way for Black to lose his queen is
5...d6 6 ♗c4 ♘f6?! (6...a6 prepares ...♘f6)
7 e5 ♘xe5?? 8 ♘xe5 dxe5? 9 ♗xf7+!.

1b) White moves

This arises from 5...d6 6 ♗c4 e6 7 0-0 a6 8
♕e2 ♗e7 9 ♖d1 ♗d7! (not 9...♘f6? 10
e5), a highly precise sequence for Black.
After 10 ♗f4 e5 11 ♗e3 ♘f6 12 ♖d2,
Black is solid, but White is active.

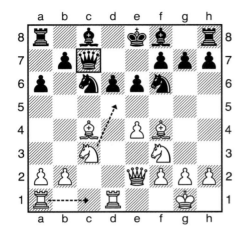

2a) Black moves

The queen is misplaced after 10...♘e5?! 11 ♗xe5 dxe5 12 ♖ac1 ♗d7? 13 ♗xe6!! fxe6 14 ♘d5, with a decisive attack. 10...♗e7 11 ♖ac1 0-0 (2b) is more solid.

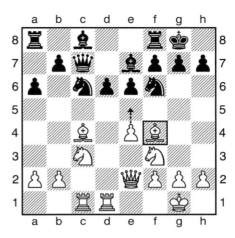

2b) White moves

12 e5?! dxe5 13 ♘xe5 ♗d6! 14 ♖xd6 ♕xd6 15 ♘g6 e5! is a nasty trap, but 12 ♗b3 ♕b8 13 e5 ♘h5 14 ♗g5 gives White typical gambit play for the pawn.

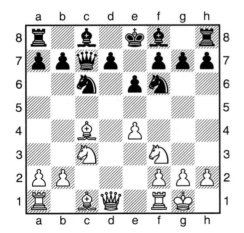

3) White moves

After 8 ♕e2?! (a standard Morra move) 8...♘g4! 9 h3?? ♘d4! White loses king or queen. 8 ♘b5 ♕b8 9 e5! is better, since 9...♘xe5? 10 ♘xe5 ♕xe5 11 ♖e1 gives White a strong attack, but 9...a6 10 exf6 axb5 allows both sides chances.

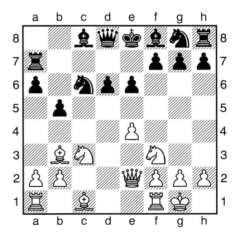

4) White moves

Black's idea is to use this rook to neutralize White's d-file play, but 10 ♖d1 ♖d7 11 ♗f4 ♗e7 12 ♖ac1 ♗b7 13 e5 gives White good play after 13...♘h6? 14 exd6 ♗xd6 15 ♗xd6 ♖xd6 16 ♘e4, 13...dxe5 14 ♘xe5 or 13...d5 14 ♘xd5! followed by e6.

♗b5 Sicilian

Healthy development with a rich choice of plans

This is yet another way to avoid the main lines of the Sicilian, but this time White relies on piece-play to start with. Like in the Ruy Lopez, the main idea is not so much to exchange pieces as to put pressure on Black. By moving to b5, White's bishop aims to tie up Black's queenside pieces, while keeping all options open with his centre pawns. For instance, he might play c3 and d4, seeking an 'ideal' centre, or try to play both c4 and d4, opening the game but keeping a 'bind' on the d5-square. There are also lines where White exchanges on c6, doubling Black's pawns, and keeps the game closed in a similar spirit to the Nimzo-Indian (see page 102). The ♗b5 lines have been used by Fischer and Kasparov, who both showed how aggressive this apparently modest idea can become.

There are two main forms of ♗b5 Sicilian: **1 e4 c5 2 ♘f3 ♘c6 3 ♗b5** *(1a)* and **1 e4 c5 2 ♘f3 d6 3 ♗b5+** *(1b)*. White needs to play something else after 1 e4 c5 2 ♘f3 e6, because 3 ♗b5 would be pointless then! One idea is 3 ♘c3, meeting 3...♘c6 with 4 ♗b5.

Basic Positions of the ♗b5 Sicilian

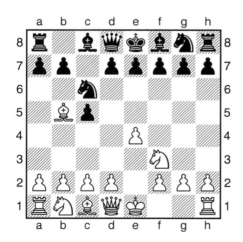

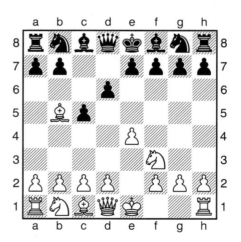

1a) Black moves

With 3...g6, Black wants to control d4, e.g. 4 ♗xc6 dxc6 *(2)*, but both sides have other strategies. 3...d6 *(5)* and 3...e6 4 ♗xc6 bxc6 *(3)* are different structures.

1b) Black moves

Now 3...♘d7 4 d4 ♘f6 5 ♘c3 cxd4 6 ♕xd4 leaves Black a little short of space, while for 3...♘c6 see diagram 5. 3...♗d7 4 ♗xd7+ ♕xd7 *(4)* is more common.

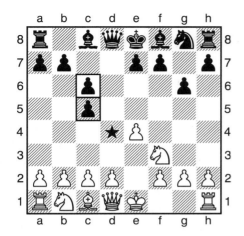

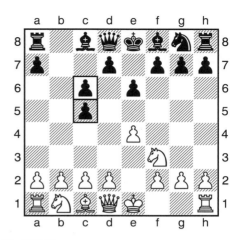

2) White moves

5 d3 ♗g7 6 h3 (6 ♘c3 ♗g4! is inconvenient) 6...e5 (a central foothold) 7 ♗e3 ♕e7 8 ♕d2 is typical. Note White's flexibility: he can attack on either flank, and his knights have many options.

3) White moves

Black can easily play the central advance ...d5, but White hopes that the doubled c-pawns will prove clumsy and weak; e.g., 5 b3 d5?! 6 d3 followed by c4 with a war of attrition like a Nimzo-Indian.

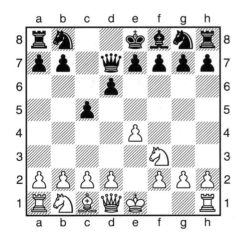

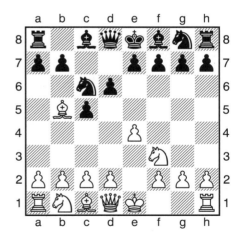

4) White moves

5 0-0 ♘f6 6 ♖e1 ♘c6 7 c3 e6 8 d4 creates a pawn-centre, but 8...d5 9 e5 ♘e4 strikes back well. 5 c4 ♘c6 6 d4 cxd4 (6...♕g4?! is a risky pawn-grab) 7 ♘xd4 ♘f6 8 ♘c3 is a kind of Maroczy Bind (page 62).

5) White moves

Note that this position can be reached from both move-orders. After 4 0-0 ♗d7 5 c3 ♘f6 6 ♖e1 a6, 7 ♗xc6 ♗xc6 8 d4 ♗xe4 9 ♗g5 is an exciting gambit, and 7 ♗a4 b5 8 ♗c2 e5 is like a Ruy Lopez!

Open Sicilian: Introduction

White picks up the gauntlet

White's most popular and aggressive option is to play **1 e4 c5 2 ♘f3** and **3 d4**, opening the centre and developing his pieces rapidly. Black will have to dig deep to defend his position against the inevitable onslaught. But if he can do so without giving too much ground, then he has great long-term prospects, with his strong central pawns and c-file play. After 2...d6 3 d4 cxd4 4 ♘xd4 ♘f6 5 ♘c3 (*1a*), 2...♘c6 3 d4 cxd4 4 ♘xd4 (*1b*) or 2...e6 3 d4 cxd4 4 ♘xd4 (*2a*), White must identify the main drawback of Black's set-up, and throw all his resources into exploiting it. This can mean an advance by any (or all!) of his kingside pawns to harass Black's pieces or storm the king's defences. Or central play with sacrifices on d5, f5 or e6 to smash open lines and rip the black king from his home on e8. Or Black might allow White a surgical liquidation to a favourable ending. Black's task is to stay flexible, make use of every chance of counterplay and to make no more positional concessions than are necessary for immediate survival.

Basic Positions of the Open Sicilian

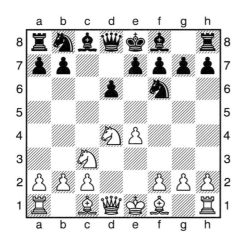
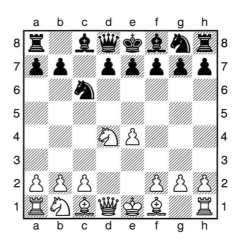

1a) Black moves

We shall see the Najdorf (5...a6) and the Dragon (5...g6) later. 5...e6 6 g4! should be compared with Najdorf lines. 5...♘c6 6 ♗g5 (*4*) keeps the pressure on Black.

1b) Black moves

4...g6 5 c4 is the Maroczy Bind, leading to slower play where Black is short of space. 4...e5 5 ♘b5 (*3*) is a sharper idea, and for 4...♘f6 5 ♘c3 e5, see page 68.

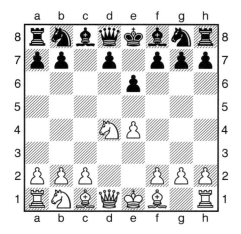

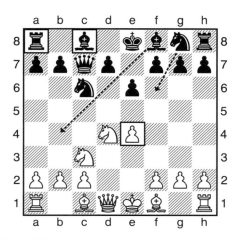

2a) Black moves

4...a6 is flexible, but so is the reply 5 ♗d3 with ideas of c4, clamping down on ...b5. 4...♘f6 5 ♘c3 ♗b4?! 6 e5 ♘e4 7 ♕g4 leads to complications. 4...♘c6 5 ♘c3 ♕c7 (2b) is safer and more popular.

2b) White moves

Black has ideas of ...♗b4 and an attack on the e4-pawn. But after 6 ♗e2 a6 7 0-0 ♘f6 (not 7...♘ge7? 8 ♘db5!!) 8 ♗e3 ♗b4, the cunning 9 ♘a4 targets Black's sleeping queenside, with sharp play.

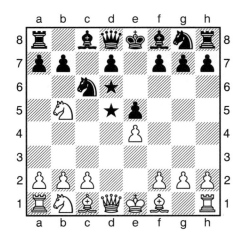

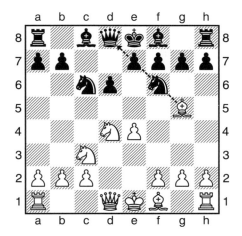

3) Black moves

Compare 5...d6 with page 68; White can play 6 c4, while Black has new options like ...♗e7-g5. An older line is 5...a6 6 ♘d6+ ♗xd6 7 ♕xd6, when 7...♕f6 8 ♕d1! ♕g6 9 ♘c3 d5!? creates chaos.

4) Black moves

White fights for control of d5, discouraging 6...e5? (which could have been the answer to 6 ♗e2) in view of 7 ♗xf6! gxf6 8 ♘f5. So 6...e6 7 ♕d2 a6 8 0-0-0 is normal, with a typical Sicilian battle.

Sicilian Dragon

Can the fire-breathing Dragon be slain?

The Dragon is one of the most uncompromising lines of the Sicilian. It is especially popular with young and ambitious players, as tactics abound. Black places his pieces on their most natural squares, fianchettoing his king's bishop and preparing to create rapid counterplay on the c-file and against the white queenside. So is **1 e4 c5 2 ♘f3 d6 3 d4 cxd4 4 ♘xd4 ♘f6 5 ♘c3 g6** *(1a)* the ideal system for Black? Unlike the Maroczy Bind (page 62), White cannot clamp down on the centre with the move c4, but he has a very dangerous alternative plan: to mate Black by exchanging off the 'Dragon' bishop and attacking along the h-file. However, to commit to this attack, White will need to place his king on the queenside, which ups the stakes as this is walking into the teeth of Black's own attack. The main lines branch out after **6 ♗e3 ♗g7 7 f3 ♘c6 8 ♕d2 0-0** *(1b)*. If White is serious about playing for mate, then 9 ♗c4 is the move, because 9 0-0-0 d5 *(4)* focuses the battle around the centre of the board. Finally, 6 ♗e2 *(5)* is solid.

Basic Positions of the Sicilian Dragon

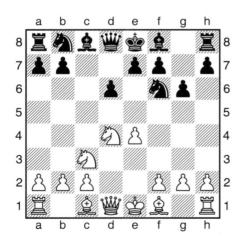

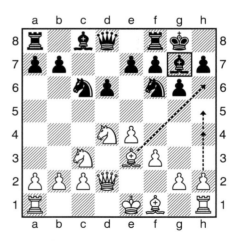

1a) White moves

White normally plays 6 ♗e3, when after ♕d2 he has the idea of exchanging off the 'Dragon' bishop by ♗h6. Note that 6...♘g4?? loses: 7 ♗b5+! ♗d7 8 ♕xg4.

1b) White moves

9 ♗c4 covers the d5-square, and pins the f7-pawn so that h4-h5xg6 would open the h-file. For 9...♗d7 10 0-0-0 ♖c8 11 ♗b3 ♘e5 see the next two diagrams.

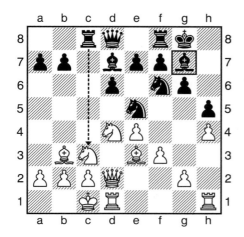

2) White moves

After 12 h4, rather than face an attack by h5 and ♗h6, Black has blocked with 12...h5. He gets counterplay after 13 ♗h6 ♗xh6 14 ♕xh6 ♖xc3 15 bxc3 ♕c8 or 13 ♗g5 ♖c5!, with ...b5 ideas.

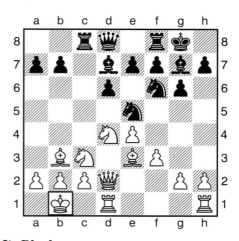

3) Black moves

White has chosen the subtle 12 ♔b1. One idea is 12...♘c4 13 ♗xc4 ♖xc4 14 g4 b5?! 15 b3! ♖c8 (15...♖c5? 16 ♘e6!!) 16 ♘dxb5 ♕a5 17 ♘d5!, as a2 is defended and 17...♕xd2 is not check.

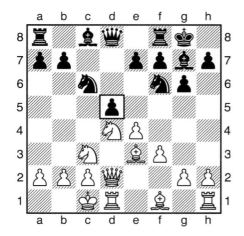

4) White moves

Black blasts open the centre, confident in his counterchances after 10 exd5 ♘xd5 11 ♘xc6 bxc6 12 ♘xd5 cxd5 13 ♕xd5 ♕c7!. A tricky line runs 10 ♔b1 ♘xd4 (not 10...dxe4?? 11 ♘xc6) 11 e5! ♘f5!.

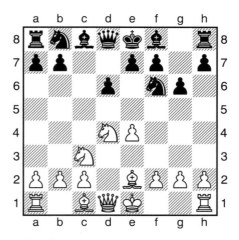

5) Black moves

The Classical Dragon. If White plays routinely, Black's central and queenside activity will be effective. Note lines like 6...♗g7 7 0-0 ♘c6 8 ♗e3 0-0 9 f4 ♕b6!, with the strong threat of 10...♘xe4.

Sicilian Najdorf

The greatest chess opening of them all?

Even if you know no other opening names, chances are you've heard of the Najdorf. It is a key battleground of modern chess, favoured by all-time greats such as Fischer and Kasparov. But the move that defines the Najdorf is, after **1 e4 c5 2 ♘f3 d6 3 d4 cxd4 4 ♘xd4 ♘f6 5 ♘c3**, the humble **5...a6** *(1a)*. What is all the fuss about? Why, of all the countless possibilities after five moves, is this one so very important? The basic point is that Black is preparing ...e5 with a useful move that prevents ♗b5+ or ♘db5. But Black is also flexible, and does not *have* to play ...e5 if White makes it unappealing with a move like 6 ♗c4 or 6 ♗g5. So Black is ready to grab the initiative, without presenting an obvious target. This adds up to a sound way for Black to play for a win – not too many openings offer that! White need not despair, as he has a great many violent options, such as 6 ♗g5 e6 7 f4 *(1b)*, planning ♕f3 and 0-0-0 and a massive attack. Another aggressive idea is 6 ♗e3 *(5)* intending f3 and g4, while the quieter 6 ♗e2 contains plenty of poison.

Basic Positions of the Sicilian Najdorf

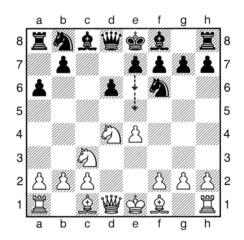

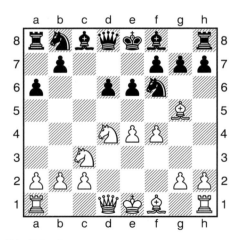

1a) White moves

Black can meet 6 ♗e2, 6 ♗e3, 6 f4 and 6 g3 with 6...e5 and develop rapidly, fighting for d5. After 6 ♗g5 and 6 ♗c4, 6...e6 keeps a grip on this key square.

1b) Black moves

The fight is on! He can try 7...b5, based on 8 e5 dxe5 9 fxe5 ♕c7 *(2)*, 7...♕b6 8 ♕d2 ♕xb2 *(3)*, or 'solid' systems such as 7...♗e7 8 ♕f3 ♕c7 9 0-0-0 ♘bd7 *(4)*.

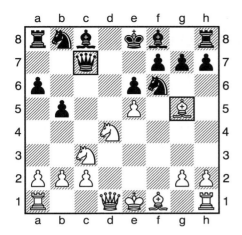

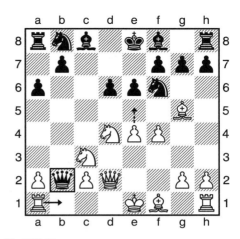

2) White moves

The tactical point 10 exf6 ♕e5+ saves Black's piece. But his development is backward, and the game is on a knife edge after 11 ♗e2 ♕xg5 12 0-0 ♖a7! 13 ♕d3 ♖d7 14 ♘e4 ♕e5 15 ♘f3 ♕xb2.

3) White moves

The famous Najdorf Poisoned Pawn. White has sacrificed the b2-pawn for attacking chances in lines like 9 ♖b1 ♕a3 10 e5 h6 11 ♗h4 dxe5 12 fxe5 ♘fd7 13 ♘e4 ♕xa2 14 ♖d1 ♕d5! 15 ♕e3 ♕xe5 16 ♗e2 ♗c5.

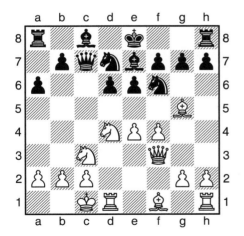

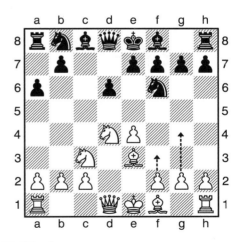

4) White moves

After 10 ♗d3, attacking plans include ♖he1 and ♘d5!?, but Black can fight for e5 by 10...h6 11 ♗h4 g5 12 fxg5 ♘e5. Another main line runs 10 g4 b5 11 ♗xf6 ♘xf6 12 g5 ♘d7 13 f5 ♘c5 14 f6.

5) Black moves

In the English Attack, White plans f3 and a kingside pawn-storm (g4-g5), and generally castles queenside. Black can choose 6...♘g4 7 ♗g5 h6, 6...e5 7 ♘b3 ♗e6 8 f3 h5!? or 6...e6 7 f3 b5 8 g4 h6.

Sveshnikov Sicilian

A rags-to-riches tale

The Sveshnikov is one of the great success stories of modern chess. It was regarded as an oddity up to the 1970s due to Black's neglect of the d5-square, but in the last twenty years it has challenged the Najdorf's 'top dog' status, and caused many players to use 'anti-Sveshnikov' move-orders such as 1 e4 c5 2 ♘c3 ♘c6 3 ♘f3 ♘f6 4 ♗b5.

This dynamic line starts with **1 e4 c5 2 ♘f3 ♘c6 3 d4 cxd4 4 ♘xd4 ♘f6 5 ♘c3 e5** *(1a)*. No slow moves here for Black – he develops rapidly and grabs a central foothold. After **6 ♘db5 d6**, Sveshnikov's key idea was to meet **7 ♗g5 a6 8 ♘a3** with **8...b5!** *(1b)*, preventing ♘c4 and threatening ...b4. It looks risky to play yet another pawn move, but Black's position works rather well. White's main attempt to lead play in a different direction is 7 ♘d5, forcing 7...♘xd5 8 exd5. While not bad for Black, this results in less dynamic play than many Sveshnikov players want. These players can try the move-order 1 e4 c5 2 ♘f3 e6 (also avoiding ♗b5 lines) 3 d4 cxd4 4 ♘xd4 ♘f6 5 ♘c3 ♘c6 *(5)*.

Basic Positions of the Sveshnikov Sicilian

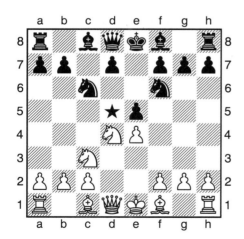

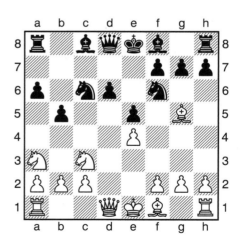

1a) White moves

Now 6 ♘f5 d5 and 6 ♘b3 ♗b4 are at least OK for Black, and 6 ♘xc6?! bxc6 even gifts him control of d5. So 6 ♘db5 d6 is normal, with a tussle over d5.

1b) White moves

Play now branches out into 9 ♘d5 ♗e7 10 ♗xf6 ♗xf6 *(2)* and 9 ♗xf6 gxf6 10 ♘d5 f5 *(3)*. In both cases it turns out that Black can play around the d5-knight.

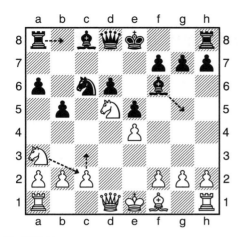

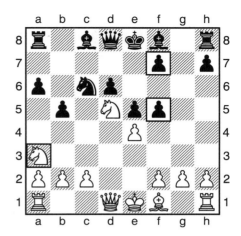

2) White moves

If White had time to play c3 and ♘c2-e3, he would have a strong grip on the position. But Black has ideas like ...♗g5, preparing to take the knight, and ...♖b8 with a well-timed ...b4 to open lines.

3) White moves

Black's pawns look messy, but the a3-knight is also poor, and Black has *two* f-pawns to attack the centre! 11 ♗d3 ♗e6 12 0-0 ♗xd5 13 exd5 ♘e7 is a solid line, and 11 ♗xb5 axb5 12 ♘xb5 *(4)* is crazy!

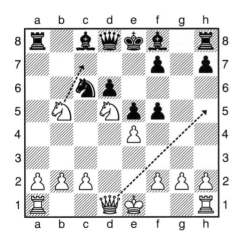

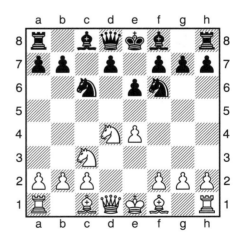

4) Black moves

This is one of many violent attacks the Sveshnikov had to survive before it became 'respectable'. 12...♖a4! 13 ♘bc7+ ♔d7 14 0-0 ♖xe4 15 ♕h5 ♘d4 keeps Black afloat by giving the king room on c6.

5) White moves

Now 6 ♘db5 d6 7 ♗f4 e5 8 ♗g5 gives us a standard Sveshnikov, avoiding White's early ♘d5 option. Cunning! But the new possibility 6 ♘xc6 bxc6 7 e5 ♘d5 8 ♘e4 gives White interesting play.

Queen's Gambit Accepted

The opening of champions

The Queen's Gambit, one of the most important openings, is defined by **1 d4 d5 2 c4**. The opening tends to be quiet, but tactics can break out unexpectedly. White wants to play 3 cxd5, and if Black responds 3...♕xd5, 4 ♘c3 attacks the queen, wins a tempo, and supports 5 e4. Black must respond to this threat. The most obvious answer is to capture the pawn by **2...dxc4** *(1a)*. This is called the Queen's Gambit Accepted. White's simplest course is 3 e3, when 3...b5?! *(2)* is a bad idea. A smarter way for Black to play is 3...♘f6 4 ♗xc4 e6 or 3...e5!?. To stop ...e5, White can play 3 ♘f3, when 3...♘f6 4 e3 e6 5 ♗xc4 c5 6 0-0 a6 *(1b)* challenges White's centre. 3 e4 is more ambitious. Then 3...♘f6 4 e5 ♘d5 5 ♗xc4 ♘b6 *(3)* targets White's backward d-pawn. Things can heat up quickly after 3...♘c6 4 ♗e3 ♘f6 5 ♘c3 e5; e.g., 6 d5 ♘a5 7 ♘f3 ♗d6! *(4)*. Finally, after 3 ♘f3 ♘f6 4 ♘c3 a6 5 e4 b5 *(5)*, Black holds the gambit pawn at the cost of allowing an attack.

Basic Positions of the Queen's Gambit Accepted

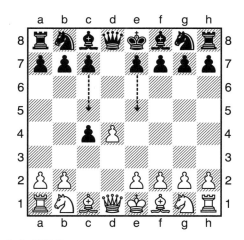

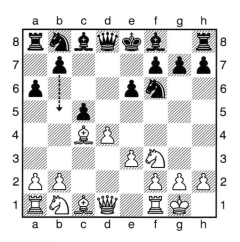

1a) White moves

Black hopes that while White is winning back his pawn, a counterblow by ...c5 will give him a fair share of the centre. The lines 3 ♘c3 e5 and 3 e4 e5 show that this is not Black's only pawn-thrust.

1b) White moves

The point of ...a6 is to prepare ...b5 and ...♗b7. So White often plays 7 a4, when 7...cxd4 8 exd4 is an isolated queen's pawn position. White has more activity but his d-pawn is vulnerable.

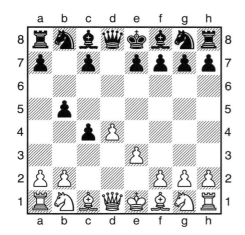

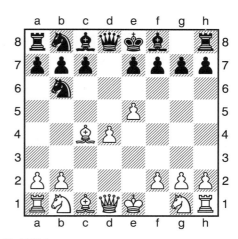

2) White moves

White attacks the b5-pawn by 4 a4!, setting the trap 4...c6?! (4...a6?! 5 axb5 and Black can't recapture) 5 axb5 cxb5?? 6 ♕f3!, when Black's rook is trapped and White wins a piece.

3) White moves

Here 6 ♗d3! is a clever retreat. For example, 6...♘c6 (not 6...♕xd4?? 7 ♗b5+, which costs Black his queen) 7 ♗e3 ♗e6 8 ♘c3 ♘b4 9 ♗e4 ♘4d5 10 ♘f3 with a space advantage for White.

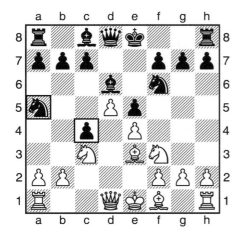

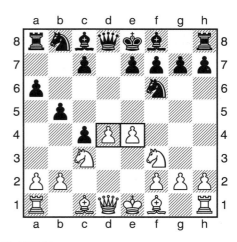

4) White moves

8 ♕a4+ looks very strong, but Black sacrifices his knight by 8...♗d7! 9 ♕xa5 a6!, when ...b6 threatens to trap the queen! After 10 ♘a4 ♕e7! 11 a3 ♘xe4 Black still intends ...b6. Tricky!

5) White moves

White, a pawn down, tries to undermine Black's position by 6 e5 ♘d5 7 a4!. Then 7...♘xc3 8 bxc3 ♕d5 (8...♗b7 9 e6!) 9 g3! ♗b7 10 ♗g2 ♕d7 11 ♗a3 makes it awkward for Black to develop.

71

<table>
<tr><td>MIGHTY
OPENING</td><td>30</td><td>Classical Queen's Gambit Declined</td></tr>
</table>

MIGHTY OPENING 30 — Classical Queen's Gambit Declined

Sometimes the old ways are the best ones

After **1 d4 d5 2 c4**, **2...e6** *(1a)* is the traditional way to decline the Queen's Gambit (we shall see the Slav, 2...c6, on page 82). Black simply shores up his important pawn on d5, even though he shuts in his queen's bishop. This was by far the most common way to play against 1 d4 in the early 20th century, and is still an extremely important opening at all levels today, although often with modern dynamic follow-ups.

One main line is 3 ♘c3 ♘f6 4 ♗g5 ♗e7 5 e3 0-0 6 ♘f3 *(1b)*. Black's traditional defences aim to simplify and free the bishop on c8. The Lasker Defence is 6...h6 7 ♗h4 ♘e4 8 ♗xe7 ♕xe7 *(2)*. The Orthodox Line, 6...♘bd7, can lead to similar play after 7 ♖c1 c6 8 ♗d3 dxc4 9 ♗xc4 ♘d5 10 ♗xe7 ♕xe7 *(3)*. Black can also reach the Orthodox via the odd-looking move 4...♘bd7 *(4)*, which invites a classic blunder. The 4...♘bd7 move-order can also lead to the Cambridge Springs Variation: 5 e3 c6 6 ♘f3 ♕a5 *(5)*.

Basic Positions of the Classical Queen's Gambit Declined

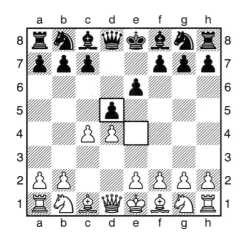

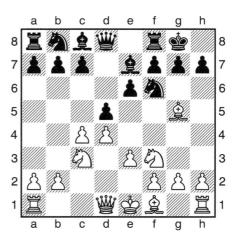

1a) White moves

White plays 3 ♘c3 to increase his influence over d5 and e4. Black generally plays 3...♘f6, to do the same (although 3...c6 is a tricky idea – see page 85). One of the key issues is the fate of the c8-bishop.

1b) Black moves

Both sides develop normally. Now Black can aim for exchanges; this was the goal pursued by the old masters. Their philosophy was that when you have less space, you should simplify.

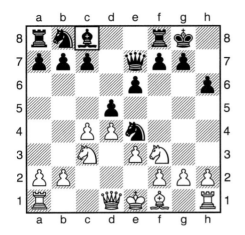

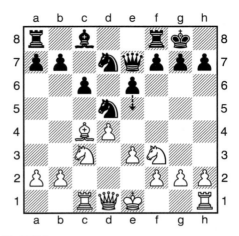

2) White moves

The Lasker Defence. One example of play is 9 ♖c1 c6 10 ♗d3 ♘xc3 11 ♖xc3 dxc4! 12 ♗xc4 ♘d7, preparing ...e5 to give Black's bishop on c8 some scope. In return, White has a bit more space.

3) White moves

Again, Black's idea is ...♘xc3 and ...e5. Aside from 11 0-0, White can avoid this by 11 ♘e4, hoping for 11...♕b4+ 12 ♕d2 ♕xd2+ 13 ♔xd2, when White has a strong centre and a space advantage.

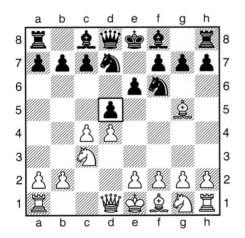

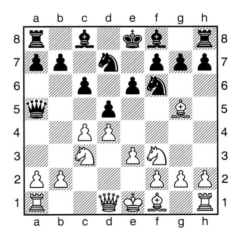

4) White moves

Can White win a pawn? Not by 5 cxd5 exd5 6 ♘xd5?? ♘xd5! 7 ♗xd8 ♗b4+, when Black wins a piece! This is one of the oldest traps in chess, and an illustration that pins can sometimes be broken.

5) White moves

7 ♘d2 stops the threat of ...♘e4, but then 7...dxc4 attacks the g5-bishop. After 8 ♗xf6 ♘xf6 9 ♘xc4 ♕c7, White has more space, but Black has the bishop-pair. 7 cxd5 ♘xd5 8 ♕d2 leads to sharper play.

Tartakower and Modern Lines

The true master is never in a hurry

After **1 d4 d5 2 c4 e6 3 ♘c3 ♘f6 4 ♘f3** *(1a)* we get a common position which can also come from the sequence 1 d4 ♘f6 2 c4 e6 3 ♘f3 d5 4 ♘c3. This can lead to the Classical lines after **4...♗e7 5 ♗g5 0-0 6 e3 h6 7 ♗h4**, but Black doesn't have to simplify by 7...♘e4 (Mighty Opening 30). The most popular move, **7...b6** *(1b)*, prepares ...♗b7 and patiently awaits developments. This is the Tartakower Variation. White can clarify the centre by 8 cxd5 ♘xd5 9 ♗xe7 ♕xe7 10 ♘xd5 exd5 *(2)* or he can enter the sophisticated line 8 ♗e2 ♗b7 9 ♗xf6!? ♗xf6 10 cxd5 exd5 *(3)*, reckoning the bishop is better on e6.

After 4...♗e7, White has the additional option of 5 ♗f4 *(4)*. Black can also vary with the Vienna Variation, 4...dxc4 5 e4 ♗b4 *(5)*, igniting a fierce fight in which specific threats dominate the play. Other possibilities are 4...c6 (see page 84) and 4...c5, the Semi-Tarrasch. Then 5 cxd5 ♘xd5 6 e4 ♘xc3 7 bxc3 is a position we examine on page 77.

Basic Positions of the Tartakower and Modern Lines

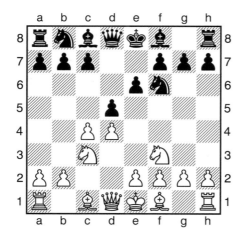

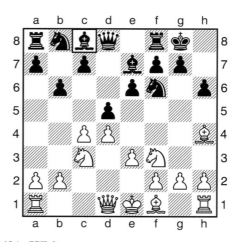

1a) Black moves

White can still choose between ♗f4 and ♗g5, but Exchange Variations are less of a worry for Black (see page 76 for the reason). He can select Classical lines or an early ...♗b4, among other options.

1b) White moves

The one piece that Black has problems with is his queen's bishop, and ...b6 gives it a place to go. White can either play directly to gain a central advantage, or try to hem in the bishop.

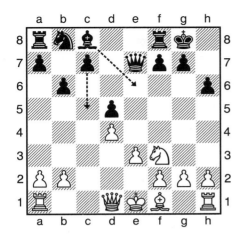

2) White moves

White can use his half-open c-file and Black's slight weaknesses on the light squares to put pressure on Black's queenside. Black can play ...♗e6 and ...c5 to establish a central presence.

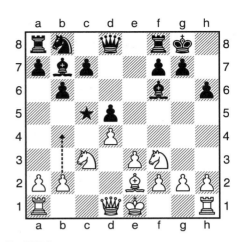

3) White moves

Black has the two bishops, but neither has much scope. White wants to prevent the position from blowing wide open and sometimes plays 11 b4 to discourage the ...c5 advance.

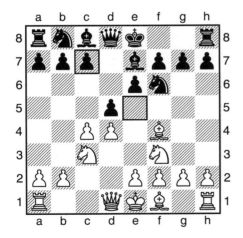

4) Black moves

White has less pressure on d5 without the option of ♗xf6. But he takes control of e5 and the bishop on f4 helps to attack Black's queenside after ♖c1 and cxd5. 5...0-0 6 e3 c5 7 dxc5 ♗xc5 8 ♕c2 ♘c6 9 a3 is normal.

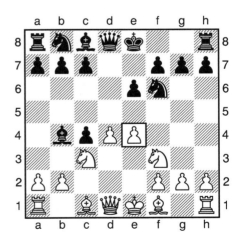

5) White moves

6 ♗g5! prevents ...♘xe4, but after 6...c5 7 ♗xc4 cxd4 8 ♘xd4 ♗xc3+ 9 bxc3 ♕a5!, Black threatens White's pawn on c3 and his bishop on g5. But 10 ♗b5+! leaves the game very far from clear.

32 Queen's Gambit Exchange Variations

To get something you have to give something

1 d4 d5 2 c4 e6 3 ♘c3 ♘f6 4 cxd5 exd5 *(1a)* is the Exchange Variation of the Queen's Gambit. Why would White give the bishop on c8 a free path, when the fundamental problem with 2...e6 is blocking in that piece? It turns out that the bishop still has a hard time finding a home, and White gets promising new ways to attack. 5 ♘f3 allows 5...c6 followed by ...♗f5 with easy development, so the main line is 5 ♗g5 ♗e7 6 e3 c6 7 ♗d3 0-0 8 ♕c2 (threatening 9 ♗xf6 and 10 ♗xh7+) 8...♘bd7 *(1b)*. Now White can play 9 ♘f3 ♖e8 10 0-0 ♘f8 *(2)* or 9 ♘ge2 ♖e8 10 0-0 ♘f8 11 f3 *(3)*. He can also castle queenside. Instead of 4...exd5, 4...♘xd5 cedes the centre to White, beginning with 5 e4 ♘xc3 6 bxc3 c5 7 ♘f3 *(4)*. But Black gets a solid position that is hard to crack. The exchange on d5 also occurs after 3...♗e7 (to avoid 4 ♗g5) 4 cxd5 (for 4 ♘f3 ♘f6 see page 74) 4...exd5 5 ♗f4. A clever attack begins with 5...c6 6 e3 ♗f5 7 g4!? ♗g6 8 h4! *(5)*.

Basic Positions of the Exchange Queen's Gambit

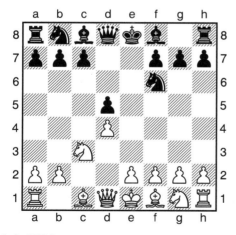

1a) White moves

The main line is 5 ♗g5 ♗e7 6 e3, when Black can't play 6...♗f5? due to 7 ♕b3!, winning a pawn. But after 6...c6, 7 ♗d3 also stops ...♗f5. So Black has no good way to develop that bishop actively.

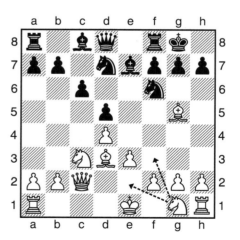

1b) White moves

Black will take the e-file by ...♖e8 and transfer his knight to f8 to secure the kingside. White must decide where to put his king's knight; his choice determines which sector he should attack in.

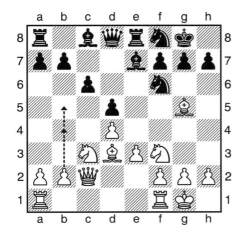

2) White moves

With the knight on f3, it's hard for White to advance in the centre, so he tends to play b4-b5, the 'minority attack'. Black can hold up that advance, but it will take time to generate kingside counterplay.

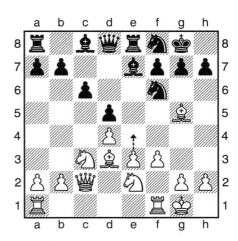

3) Black moves

With the pawn on f3, the plan is to expand in the centre by e4, and possibly e5 followed by f4-f5. Black will counter this with ...c5 at some point, and/or pointing his pieces at White's king by ...♗d6.

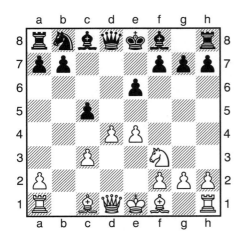

4) Black moves

White owns the centre, so Black develops by 7...cxd4 8 cxd4 ♗b4+ 9 ♗d2 ♗xd2+ 10 ♕xd2 0-0. White follows with ♗c4, 0-0 and ♖ad1, while Black plays ...b6 and ...♗b7 with a solid game.

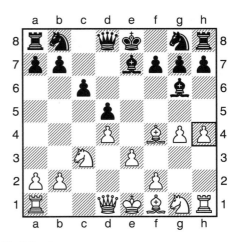

5) Black moves

White threatens 9 h5 ♗e4 10 f3, trapping Black's bishop, and 8...♗xh4? loses to 9 ♕b3! b6 10 ♖xh4! ♕xh4 11 ♘xd5! cxd5 12 ♗b5+. The Queen's Gambit doesn't always lead to slow play!

Tarrasch Defence

The isolated pawn – weak or strong?

1 d4 d5 2 c4 e6 3 ♘c3 c5 *(1a)* is the Tarrasch Defence to the Queen's Gambit, a radical attempt to break White's central pressure. White can often force an isolated pawn upon his opponent, but in return faces Black's active pieces. In the main line, 4 cxd5 exd5 5 ♘f3 ♘c6 6 g3 ♘f6 7 ♗g2 ♗e7 8 0-0 0-0 *(1b)*, White aims his g2-bishop at the d5-pawn. In this line, 6...c4 *(2)* avoids the isolated pawn but also releases the pressure on White's centre. But let's step back a few more moves. What happens if White plays 5 dxc5 to win a pawn? Then the tactical 5...d4 6 ♘a4 b5! 7 cxb6 axb6 *(3)* gives Black the initiative. One move earlier, Black can try the daring gambit 4...cxd4!? 5 ♕xd4 ♘c6 *(4)*.

The modest 4 e3 is called the Symmetrical Tarrasch. Then 4...♘f6 5 ♘f3 ♘c6 *(5)* is a position that can also arise from the Semi-Tarrasch (page 74). Here either player can end up with an isolated queen's pawn; e.g., 6 ♗d3 cxd4 7 exd4 dxc4 8 ♗xc4.

Basic Positions of the Tarrasch Defence

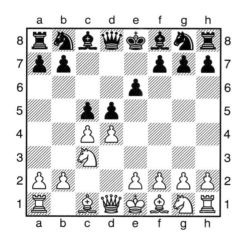

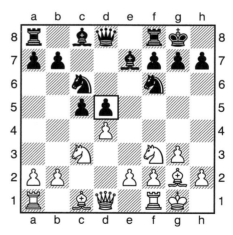

1a) White moves

Black wants to free his pieces and gain a share of the centre, so he lashes out by attacking d4. White has to react quickly, but with a second piece coming out soon, he is ready for a battle in the centre.

1b) White moves

The usual moves 9 ♗g5 cxd4 10 ♘xd4 set up the isolated d-pawn. White can attack it directly, or he can play ♘xc6 and try to exploit Black's backward c6-pawn with his rook on the c-file.

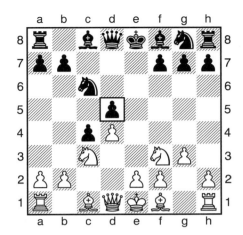

2) White moves

Here White will try to attack the d5 point, and Black to defend it. The sequence 7 ♗g2 ♗b4 8 0-0 ♘ge7 is normal, and now White can force the pace with 9 e4!, blasting open the centre.

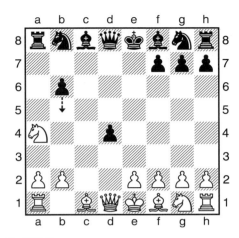

3) White moves

Black threatens ...b5, winning the wayward knight. Wild tactics often result; e.g., 8 e3 ♗d7 9 b3 b5 10 ♘b2 ♗b4+ 11 ♗d2 and now 11...dxe3! 12 ♗xb4 ♕h4!, when Black gets his piece back.

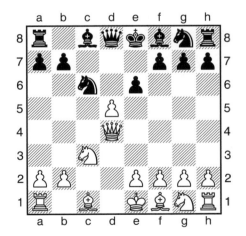

4) White moves

After 6 ♕d1 exd5 7 ♕xd5 ♗d7, Black will gain more time by ...♘f6, and follow up by ...♗c5, ...♕e7 and ...0-0-0 with attacking chances. But White has no weaknesses, so is it worth a pawn?

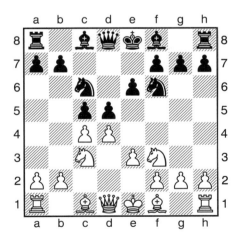

5) White moves

One way to unbalance this position is 6 cxd5 exd5 7 ♗b5. Then 7...♗d6 8 dxc5 ♗xc5 9 0-0 0-0 is a standard isolated pawn position of a type which you see in many other openings.

Sometimes the best defence is a good offence

After **1 d4 d5 2 c4**, Black has a number of unusual and aggressive ideas. The most popular is **2...♘c6** *(1a)*, the Chigorin Defence, which is based upon quick development. One main line is 3 ♘f3 ♗g4 4 cxd5 ♗xf3 5 dxc6 ♗xc6 6 ♘c3 e6 7 e4 ♗b4 *(2)*. Also typical is 3 cxd5 ♕xd5 4 e3 e5 5 ♘c3 ♗b4 6 ♗d2 ♗xc3 7 bxc3 (7 ♗xc3!? is another idea) 7...♘ge7 *(3)*, when White has the bishop-pair. In both cases, White's big and potentially mobile centre requires a dynamic reaction by Black. After 3 ♘c3 dxc4 4 ♘f3, Black must avoid 4...♗g4? 5 d5 ♗xf3 6 exf3! ♘e5 7 ♗f4! ♘g6 8 ♗xc4! ♘xf4 9 ♗b5+.

The Albin Counter-Gambit begins with **2...e5** *(1b)*. It gives up a pawn in return for activity. After 3 dxe5 d4, many players have fallen for an entertaining trap which follows 4 e3?! ♗b4+ 5 ♗d2 *(4)*. The traditional main line goes 4 ♘f3 ♘c6 5 g3 ♗g4 6 ♗g2 ♕d7 7 0-0 0-0-0 *(5)*, when both sides directly attack the enemy king.

Basic Positions of the Chigorin Defence and Albin Counter-Gambit

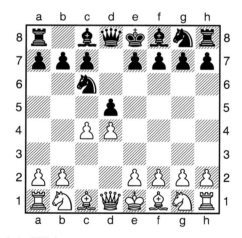

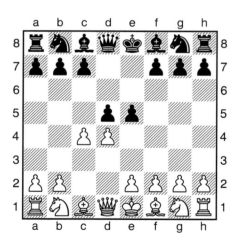

1a) White moves

Black develops quickly and attacks d4. He also supports the central thrust ...e5, but the freeing move ...c5, often a key idea in the Queen's Gambit, is eliminated. White can grab space, but must be careful.

1b) White moves

Black's bold challenge in the centre is based upon the pawn sacrifice 3 dxe5 d4!, when his advanced pawn cramps White's development and the pawn on e5 can often be attacked and recovered.

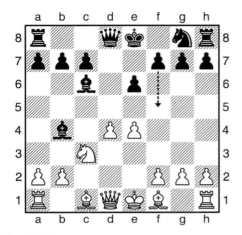

2) White moves

A typical main line. White has the ideal centre and free development, but Black has pressure on e4. The move ...f5 is a thematic idea, intending to crack open the long light-square diagonal.

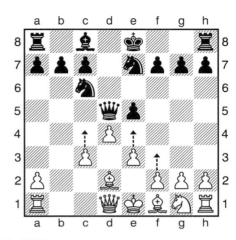

3) White moves

Black's rapid piece development certainly looks impressive, but White can sometimes get a superior game by expanding in the centre by c4 or f3 and e4. Then his two bishops will become more effective.

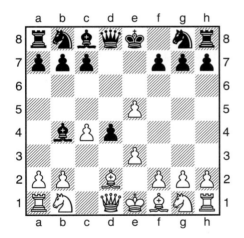

4) Black moves

5...dxe3! is strong: 6 ♗xb4?? (a blunder, but 6 fxe3 leaves weak pawns on e5 and e3) 6...exf2+ 7 ♔e2 fxg1♘+! (an unusual promotion). Now 8 ♖xg1 loses to 8...♗g4+, and 8 ♔e1 ♕h4+ is killing.

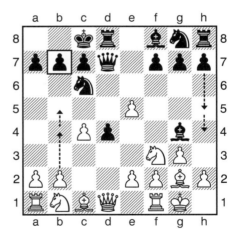

5) White moves

The battle lines are drawn: Black can attack by ...♗h3 and ...h5-h4, and White with b4-b5. A cute trick is 8 ♕b3 ♗h3? 9 e6! ♗xe6 10 ♘e5!, attacking and damaging Black's queenside.

81

Slav

So solid, it's actually aggressive!

The Slav is a very solid reply to the Queen's Gambit. Black answers **1 d4 d5 2 c4** with **2...c6** *(1a)*, which has similar motivations to the Caro-Kann – supporting the d5-pawn without blocking in the queen's bishop. A further idea is that soon Black may play ...dxc4 intending ...b5 with a solid extra pawn. Note that if White exchanges pawns, by 3 cxd5 cxd5, the position is completely symmetrical (unlike the lines we saw on page 76), and can be drawish unless either side makes a serious error or goes to extreme efforts to break the deadlock – you may view that as a good thing or a bad thing!

The main line runs 3 ♘f3 ♘f6 4 ♘c3, when Black has a major choice. 4...e6 is the Semi-Slav (page 84), while the odd-looking 4...a6 *(4)* is a highly popular sideline and 4...dxc4 (intending ...b5) 5 a4 *(1b)* is more traditional. 3 ♘f3 ♘f6 4 e3 ♗f5 gives Black solid development, but 3 ♘c3 ♘f6 4 e3 *(5)* is another plan, trying to take the sting out of Black's ...dxc4 idea. But 3 ♘c3 also gives Black ideas like 3...e5, an exciting gambit.

Basic Positions of the Slav

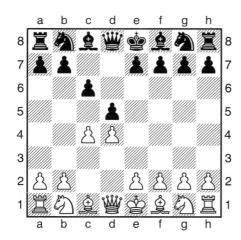

1a) White moves

Although basically solid, the Slav can lead to very sharp, violent battles. If White wants to avoid drawish equality, he must play vigorously and take risks.

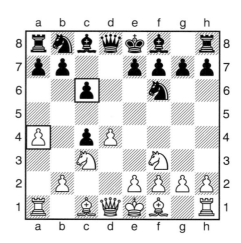

1b) Black moves

White makes sure he regains his pawn, but his move a4 may prove no more useful than Black's ...c6. Now 5...♗f5 covers e4 – see the next two diagrams.

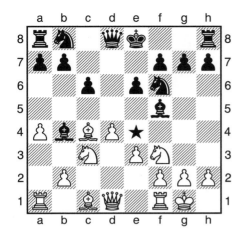

2) Black moves

6 e3 e6 7 ♗xc4 ♗b4 8 0-0 brings us to this standard position. Note the battle for control of e4. After 8...0-0 9 ♕e2 ♘bd7 10 e4 ♗g6 White's centre is under fire, and he will soon be forced to play e5.

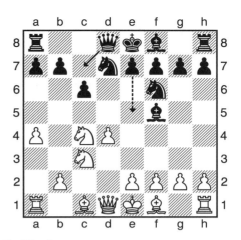

3) Black moves

This is the position after 6 ♘e5 ♘bd7 7 ♘xc4, a more ambitious approach intending f3 and e4. Black can hit back by 7...♕c7 8 g3! e5! 9 dxe5 ♘xe5 10 ♗f4 ♘fd7 11 ♗g2 g5!?, with complex play.

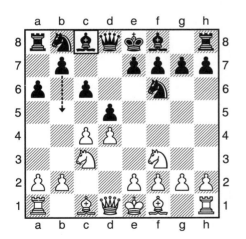

4) White moves

Black plans ...b5, forcing a decision from the c4-pawn. 5 cxd5 cxd5 gives the knight the c6-square, and 5 e3 b5 6 b3 ♗g4 is fine for Black, so White tends to play 5 c5, when ...e5 is an idea for Black to prepare.

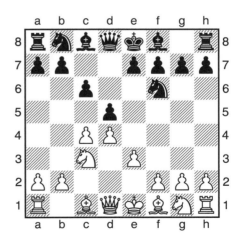

5) Black moves

4...♗f5?! 5 cxd5 cxd5 6 ♕b3 highlights the weakness of b7, so Black should try another approach. 4...g6 is a slow form of Grünfeld, 4...e6 5 ♘f3 is a Semi-Slav, and 4...a6 is again possible here.

83

Semi-Slav

Much more than half a Slav!

The Semi-Slav refers to the position after **1 d4 d5 2 c4 c6 3 ♘f3 ♘f6 4 ♘c3 e6** *(1a)*, which can be reached from a large number of different move-orders. Black chooses a sequence based on which sidelines he wishes to avoid. For instance, if he doesn't like 1 d4 d5 2 c4 c6 3 cxd5, he might play 1 d4 d5 2 c4 e6 3 ♘c3 c6 *(5)*. Or 1 d4 ♘f6 2 c4 e6, intending 3 ♘f3 d5 4 ♘c3 c6, and choosing a Nimzo-Indian if White plays 3 ♘c3. So the Semi-Slav can only be seen as part of a repertoire, rather than a complete defence.

But what an opening it is! Despite its passive appearance (are ...e6 and ...c6 really counterattacking moves?), the Semi-Slav is one of the most ambitious and complex opening systems of all, and the scene for some of the greatest chess battles of all time. Why? ...dxc4 is definitely a threat now, and 5 a4 is insipid when Black hasn't already played ...dxc4, while 5 ♗g5 *(4)* and 5 e3 ♘bd7 6 ♗d3 dxc4 7 ♗xc4 b5 8 ♗d3 *(1b)* both allow Black to create enormous complications and a highly unbalanced middlegame.

Basic Positions of the Semi-Slav

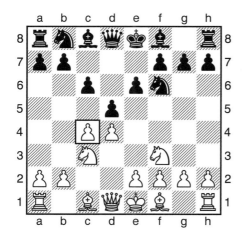

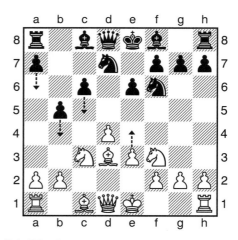

1a) White moves

5 e3 covers c4 directly, while 5 ♗g5 is a tactical defence, meeting 5...dxc4 with 6 e4, threatening 7 e5. 5 cxd5 exd5 allows Black easy development with ...♗f5.

1b) Black moves

This is known as the Meran. Black is active on the queenside, so White needs to gain ground in the centre. This leads to fireworks – see the next two diagrams.

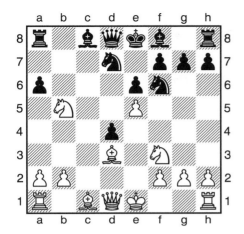

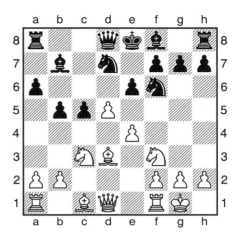

2) Black moves

The board is on fire! This is the situation after 8...a6 9 e4 c5 10 e5 cxd4 11 ♘xb5. Danger abounds for both sides. For instance, 11...axb5 12 exf6 gxf6 13 0-0 ♕b6 guarantees safety for neither king.

3) Black moves

Play here, after 8...♗b7 9 0-0 a6 10 e4 c5 11 d5, is strategically complex. Black dare not open the e-file with his king so exposed, but 11...♕c7 12 dxe6 fxe6 13 ♗c2 leads to a tense boardwide battle.

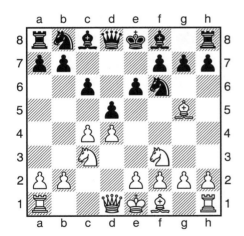

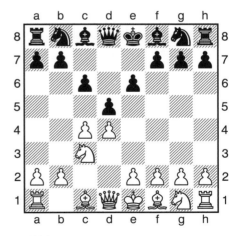

4) Black moves

This leads to the sharpest play. 5...dxc4 6 e4 b5 7 e5 h6 8 ♗h4 g5 9 ♘xg5 hxg5 10 ♗xg5 is a chaotic mess, while 5...h6 6 ♗h4!? (6 ♗xf6 is simpler) 6...dxc4 7 e4 g5 8 ♗g3 b5 is an exciting gambit line.

5) White moves

Both sides can avoid a normal Semi-Slav. 4 e4 dxe4 5 ♘xe4 ♗b4+ 6 ♗d2!? is a sharp gambit, while 4 ♘f3 dxc4 5 e3 b5 6 a4 ♗b4 leads to complex play. And 4 e3 f5!? is a kind of Stonewall Dutch.

London, Colle and Trompowsky

Following the paths less-travelled

After **1 d4 d5**, White doesn't have to play a Queen's Gambit with 2 c4. **2 ♘f3** *(1a)* is a solid option, which can also arise from 1 ♘f3 d5 2 d4. Black is free from central pressure, so he can safely play moves such as 2...c5, 2...♗f5 or 2...c6. However, the flexible **2...♘f6** is most common. Then **3 ♗f4** is called the London System; one important line goes 3...e6 4 e3 c5 5 c3 (to answer 5...♕b6 with 6 ♕b3) 5...♘c6 6 ♘bd2 ♗d6 *(2)*. The Colle System is **3 e3**, when after 3...e6 4 ♗d3 c5 the main lines are 5 b3 ♘c6 6 0-0 ♗d6 7 ♗b2 0-0 and 5 c3 ♘c6 6 ♘bd2 ♗d6 7 0-0 0-0 *(3)*. A unique position arises after 3...♗f5 4 ♗d3 e6!? (4...♗g6 is also OK) 5 ♗xf5 exf5 *(4)*.

Another opening without c4 is **1 d4 ♘f6 2 ♗g5** *(1b)*, known as the Trompowsky Attack. Hitting the bishop with 2...♘e4 is a popular response, when 3 ♗f4 c5 can be met by the safe 4 f3 or the trickier 4 d5 *(5)*. Play is often tactical, with many structures possible.

Basic Positions of the London, Colle and Trompowsky

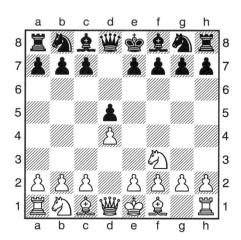

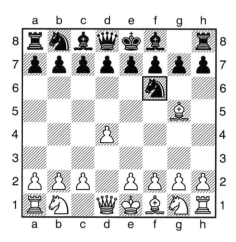

1a) Black moves

White adds to his control of d4 and e5. Assuming that he doesn't play the sharp move c4 next, the main drawback is that he doesn't attack the pawn on d5, so Black can develop freely.

1b) Black moves

White intends ♗xf6, doubling Black's pawns, and meets 2...e6 by 3 e4 h6 4 ♗xf6. Then Black obtains the advantage of the bishop-pair, but White has more space, an ideal centre and very active knights.

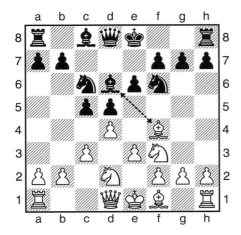

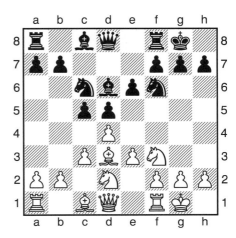

2) White moves

Here White can exchange bishops by 7 ♗xd6, but this helps Black to achieve his freeing move ...e5 quickly. 7 ♗g3 hopes for 7...♗xg3 8 hxg3 with a half-open h-file; instead, 7...0-0 8 ♗d3 ♕e7 is safer.

3) White moves

White often plays 8 dxc5 ♗xc5 9 e4, when Black needs to avoid the classic ♗xh7+ trap. For example, 9...♗d7?! 10 e5 ♘e8 11 ♘b3 ♗b6? 12 ♗xh7+! ♔xh7 13 ♘g5+ with a powerful attack.

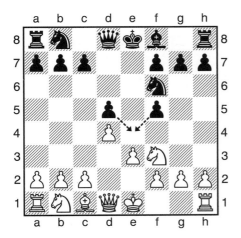

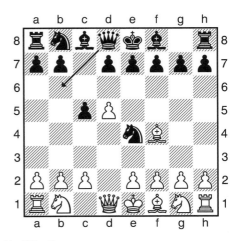

4) White moves

Black's pawns are doubled, but he gets a half-open e-file and clamps down on e4. White's bishop will be hard to activate. True, 6 ♕d3 threatens both ♕xf5 and ♕b5+, but then 6...♕c8! is quite safe.

5) Black moves

White has more space, but Black has the tricky 4...♕b6, with the idea 5 b3?? ♕f6! or 5 ♕c1?! c4 6 e3 ♕a5+ 7 c3 ♕xd5. Here 5 ♘d2 ♕xb2 6 ♘xe4 ♕b4+ 7 ♕d2 ♕xe4 8 e3 is an unclear gambit, while 5 ♗c1 is safe.

Dutch Defence

What the Sicilian sees when it looks in a mirror?

By meeting **1 d4** with **1...f5** *(1a)*, Black rejects all ideas of playing for simple equality by keeping the position symmetrical. However, by staking a claim to the central square e4, he also ensures that White cannot easily gain a strong pawn-centre by advancing his pawn to that square. Alert readers will have noticed that the Dutch Defence is a kind of mirror-image Sicilian Defence. But while these openings share some ideas, the play is very different. In the Dutch, Black normally castles kingside, and often attacks on that side of board. In the Sicilian, White can easily play d4, but here the mirror-image idea of playing e4 is more difficult for White as he has less control over this square.

When masters face the Dutch, they normally play 2 g3 ♘f6 3 ♗g2 *(1b)* followed by further flexible development. Black can try to storm this set-up, but central play is often safer and better. White has plenty of other ideas, including gambits such as 2 e4 *(4)* or 2 g4 and piece-play with moves like 2 ♗g5 *(5)* or 2 ♘c3.

Basic Positions of the Dutch Defence

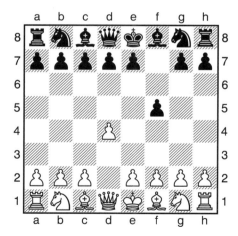

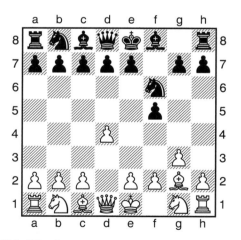

1a) White moves

Black must play carefully in the next few moves, as his king is more exposed than in most openings. 2 g4 fxg4 3 h3 is safely met by 3...g3, keeping lines closed.

1b) Black moves

Black's main set-ups are now ...g6 and ...♗g7 (Leningrad), ...e6 and ...d5 (Stonewall), or ...e6 and ...d6 (Classical). White will play ♘h3 or ♘f3 and castle.

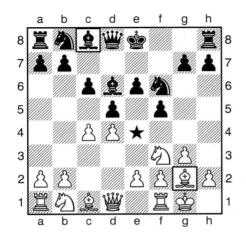

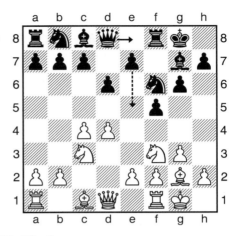

2) White moves

This Stonewall comes from 3...e6 4 c4 c6 5 ♘f3 d5 6 0-0 ♗d6. White can exchange bishops by 7 ♗f4 or 7 b3 and ♗a3, but Black's 'bad' bishop can be highly effective on a6, b7 or even h5 (via d7 and e8).

3) Black moves

3...g6 4 ♘f3 ♗g7 5 0-0 0-0 6 c4 d6 7 ♘c3 reaches this Leningrad set-up. 7...♕e8 prepares ...e5. 8 ♖e1 intends e4, but 8...♕f7 shows Black's teeth: the queen attacks c4 and puts potential pressure on f2.

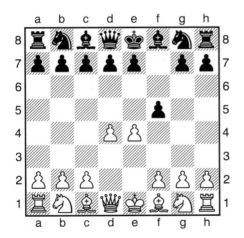

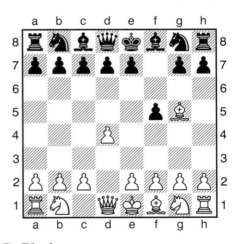

4) Black moves

This is the Staunton Gambit. After 2...fxe4 3 ♘c3 ♘f6 (not 3...d5? 4 ♕h5+), 4 f3 d5! gives White little (4...exf3?! 5 ♘xf3 is perilous), while 4 ♗g5 ♘c6! 5 d5 ♘e5 6 ♕d4 ♘f7 is perfectly OK for Black.

5) Black moves

White's main idea is that 2...♘f6 3 ♗xf6 awkwardly doubles Black's pawns. After 2...g6 3 ♘d2 White intends e4, while 2...h6 is risky; e.g., 3 ♗h4 g5 (trapping the bishop?) 4 e4! threatens ♕h5#.

Black fights for the initiative right away!

These two openings both begin with **1 d4 ♘f6 2 c4 c5**, attacking White's centre without delay. An exchange of pawns would leave Black with a central pawn-majority, so White almost always replies **3 d5**, claiming a space advantage. The Modern Benoni is **3...e6 4 ♘c3 exd5 5 cxd5 d6** *(1a)*, with Black intending ...g6 and ...♗g7. After 6 e4 g6, the traditional Main Line is 7 ♘f3 ♗g7 8 ♗e2 0-0 9 0-0. Black would like to play ...b5 and White to achieve e5, but after 9...a6 10 a4 ♗g4 11 ♗f4 ♗xf3 12 ♗xf3 ♕e7 and ...♘bd7, both of these plans are frustrated for now. Instead of 8 ♗e2, a modern scheme is 8 h3 (preventing ...♗g4) 8...0-0 9 ♗d3, when Black can lash out with 9...b5!? *(2)*. White himself can adopt more radical approaches, most notably 7 f4 ♗g7 8 ♗b5+ *(3)*.

The Benko Gambit, **3...b5!?** *(1b)*, is a bold pawn offer. The most common line is 4 cxb5 a6 5 bxa6 g6 6 ♘c3 ♗xa6 *(4)*. A good illustration of what Black is trying to do is 7 e4 ♗xf1 8 ♔xf1 d6 9 ♘f3 ♗g7 10 g3 0-0 11 ♔g2 ♘bd7 12 ♖e1 ♕a5 13 ♖e2 ♖fb8 *(5)*.

Basic Positions of the Modern Benoni and Benko Gambit

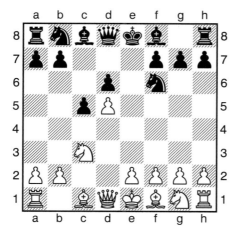

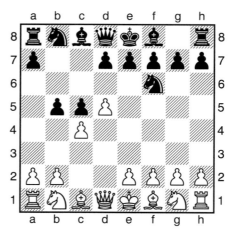

1a) White moves

The unbalanced structure suggests plans for both sides: White advances his centre pawns, while Black counters on the queenside. The play is highly tactical.

1b) White moves

This gambit is unlike others we have seen. If White accepts the pawn, Black gets slightly faster development, a weakness-free game and long-term pressure.

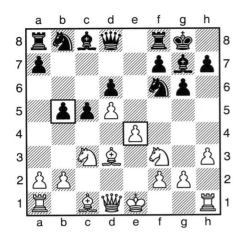

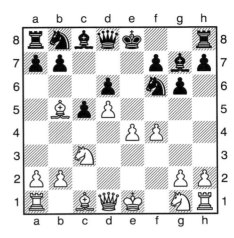

2) White moves

Black has played the desired ...b5, based on a tactical trick: 10 ♗xb5 (10 ♘xb5 ♖e8 targets e4) 10...♘xe4! 11 ♘xe4 ♕a5+ and Black recovers his piece (due to 12 ♘c3? ♗xc3+ 13 bxc3 ♕xb5) with unclear play.

3) Black moves

Since both 8...♗d7?! and 8...♘bd7 allow White his desired 9 e5, Black usually retreats by 8...♘fd7, intending ...a6 and ...b5. White can stop that with 9 a4, when both sides must form new plans.

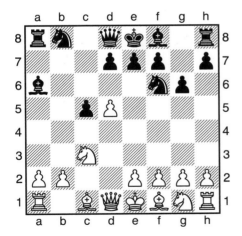

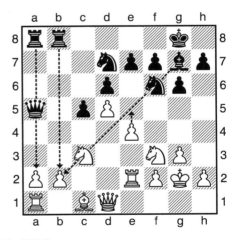

4) White moves

Black's idea is not to checkmate White or win the pawn back, but to exert pressure on the queenside by using his g7-bishop and half-open a- and b-files. It's also a little awkward for White to castle.

5) White moves

Here we see a sort of ideal position for Black, in which White has also played logically and holds on to his extra pawn. The knight on f6 may enter the fray by ...♘e8-c7 or ...♘g4-e5.

91

King's Indian: Introduction

Trench warfare – with explosions aplenty!

The King's Indian is a true fighter's opening. Giving barely a thought to any notions of 'playing for equality', Black seeks to create imbalance and to fight for the initiative straight from the opening. Often the centre becomes blocked with interlocked pawn-chains, and Black launches a massive kingside attack while White tries to break through on the other side of the board. However, many other possible types of game can arise.

The King's Indian is as much a set-up as an exact sequence of moves. Black plays ...♘f6, ...g6 and ...♗g7, and normally ...d6 and ...0-0. He allows White to play both d4 and e4, but insists that he plays c4 and ♘c3 before making the e4 advance. A standard sequence is **1 d4 ♘f6 2 c4 g6 3 ♘c3 ♗g7** *(1a)*, when 4 e4 d6 (see diagrams 2-5) gives White a massive pawn-centre, but Black hopes that it will also be a target. One way to strike at this target is ...c5 (a Benoni approach), but ...e5 is more normal. If White ends up playing d5, then Black's natural plan is kingside expansion starting with ...f5.

Basic Positions of the King's Indian Defence

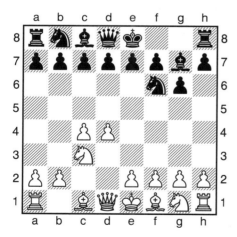

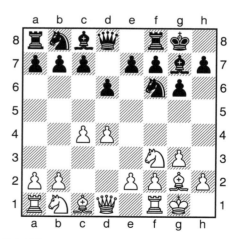

1a) White moves
White can occupy the centre and develop however he wishes. Black will soon hit back with ...e5 or ...c5 and claim that White's pawn moves have wasted time.

1b) Black moves
In this version of the King's Indian, White doesn't occupy the centre so fast. After 6...♘bd7 7 ♘c3 e5, Black has ideas of pushing on with ...e4 himself.

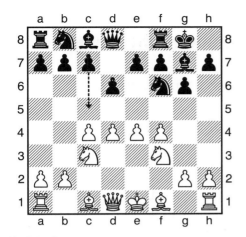

2) Black moves

In the Four Pawns Attack, White grabs the centre with both hands by 5 f4 0-0 6 ♘f3. Black can hit back by 6...c5, meeting 7 dxc5 with 7...♕a5 (e.g. 8 cxd6? ♘xe4), while 7 d5 e6 is like a Benoni.

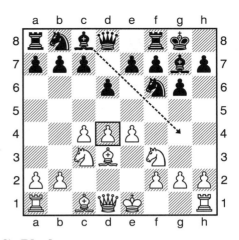

3) Black moves

White has carelessly played 5 ♗d3 0-0 6 ♘f3?! (6 ♘ge2 is better). 6...♗g4! shows that White has neglected the d4-square, and 7 h3 ♗xf3 8 ♕xf3 ♘c6 9 ♗e3 ♘d7 10 ♘e2?? ♘de5! exploits this.

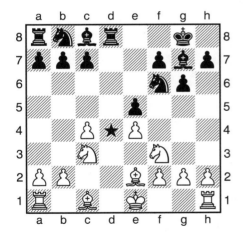

4) White moves

The Exchange Variation, 5 ♘f3 0-0 6 ♗e2 e5 7 dxe5 dxe5 8 ♕xd8 ♖xd8, is an attempt to take the fun out of the King's Indian. But even here, Black can hope to make use of the weak d4-square.

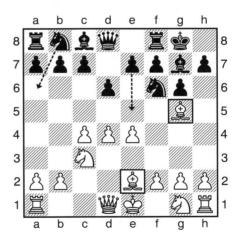

5) Black moves

5 ♗e2 0-0 6 ♗g5 is a flexible idea that sets a trap: 6...e5?? 7 dxe5 dxe5 8 ♕xd8 ♖xd8 9 ♗xf6 ♗xf6 10 ♘d5 costs Black material. He does better to play 6...♘a6 before ...e5, and 6...c5 is OK too.

King's Indian: Main Lines

The irresistible force strikes the immovable object

After **1 d4 ♘f6 2 c4 g6 3 ♘c3 ♗g7 4 e4 d6** *(1a)*, it is time for White to decide how to develop his pieces. There seem to be many ways to do so, whereas Black's options are apparently more limited. However, White must be a little careful, as the d4-square can easily become weak, while he needs to avoid his pieces blocking each other. The most popular and harmonious systems are the Sämisch and the Classical. In the Sämisch, White plays 5 f3 0-0 6 ♗e3 *(5)* and chooses his next few moves based on how Black replies (♕d2, ♘ge2 and ♗d3 are common). The Classical features 5 ♘f3 0-0 6 ♗e2. Exotic moves like 6...♘c6 and 6...♗g4 achieve little against this solid set-up, and 6...c5 7 0-0 cxd4 8 ♘xd4 gives White a pleasant Maroczy Bind. So 6...e5 *(1b)* is the traditional answer, when the question is how the central tension will be resolved: White may exchange (7 dxe5 – see page 93), advance (7 d5), or leave Black to decide whether to exchange on d4. After 7 0-0, the most popular is to force the issue with 7...♘c6 8 d5 ♘e7 *(3)*.

Basic Positions of the King's Indian Main Lines

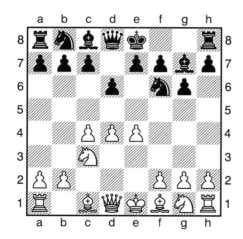

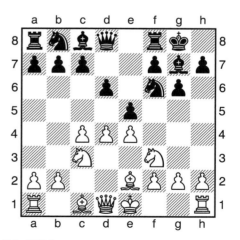

1a) White moves
White needs to develop flexibly, with a good reply in mind to each of Black's plans, most of all the ...e5 thrust. First d4 and later e4 are likely to come under fire.

1b) White moves
7 d5 stakes out a space advantage, but gives Black's knight the c5-square. 7 0-0 keeps the tension, and after 7...exd4 8 ♘xd4 Black has little true counterplay.

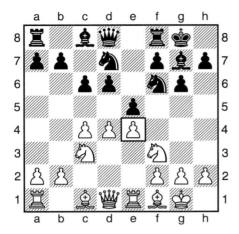

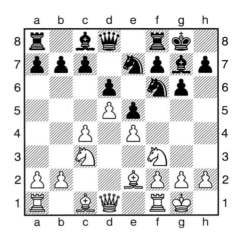

2) Black moves

7 0-0 ♘bd7 8 ♖e1 c6 9 ♗f1 has been played. Both sides are choosing useful moves however the central tension is resolved. Note White's control of e4.

3) White moves

White will attack on the queenside, and Black will gun for the white king. 9 b4 ♘h5 is one possibility, but White often regroups by 9 ♘e1 ♘d7 10 ♘d3 *(4)*.

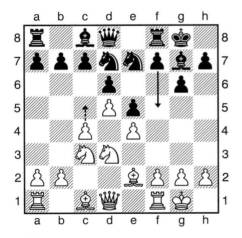

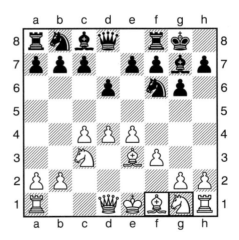

4) Black moves

White prepares the c5 advance, and 10...f5 11 ♗d2 ♘f6 (11...f4?! 12 ♗g4!) 12 f3 gives Black a problem. 12...f4 13 g4! leaves his attack stymied, but he can play 12...♔h8, keeping more plans open, such as ...♘eg8 & ...♗h6, or ...h5 & ...f4.

5) Black moves

White has supported e4 with his f-pawn without making manoeuvres like ♘f3-e1. 6...♘c6 7 ♗d3?! (7 ♘ge2 blocks the bishop but is better) 7...e5 8 ♘ge2? ♘g4! shows a drawback. 6...e5 7 d5 is another approach, as is the pawn sacrifice 6...c5!?.

95

Grünfeld Defence: Introduction

For players who love attacking pawn-centres

Although closely related to the King's Indian, the Grünfeld is a completely different animal. Black starts out like in the King's Indian with ...♘f6 and ...g6. But then, just before White can play e4, Black plays ...d5. The standard sequence is **1 d4 ♘f6 2 c4 g6 3 ♘c3 d5** *(1a)*. It might seem that the idea is to prevent White from building an 'ideal' pawn-centre, except that after 4 cxd5 ♘xd5 5 e4, White has done precisely that, and has a central majority too. In fact, Black's plan is to entice White's pawns forward and attack them, as we see after 5...♘xc3 (this exchange is the reason Black waited for White to develop his knight before playing ...d5) 6 bxc3 ♗g7 7 ♘f3 c5. All the black pieces can add to the attack against d4, with ...♗g4, ...♕a5 and ...♘c6 being useful ideas.

The critical difference from the King's Indian is that the centre is unlikely to become blocked, and there is immediate cut-and-thrust between the two armies. However, this sometimes means that there are exchanges and an early simplification into an endgame.

Basic Positions of the Grünfeld Defence

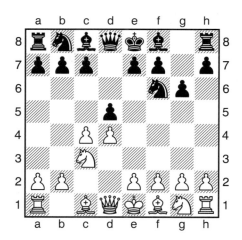

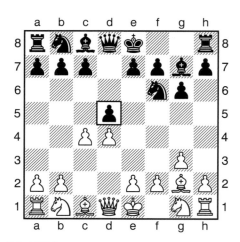

1a) White moves

We look at 4 cxd5 in the next section. White can also undermine the d5-pawn by 4 ♗g5 (hitting its protector) or attack it with 4 ♘f3 ♗g7 5 ♕b3 *(4)*.

1b) White moves

Another type of Grünfeld. White chose 3 g3 ♗g7 4 ♗g2, but Black replied 4...d5 anyway. After 5 cxd5 ♘xd5 6 e4 ♘b4, Black threatens to win the d4-pawn.

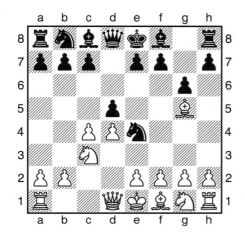

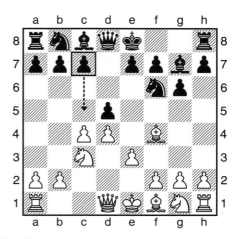

2) White moves

The position after 4 ♗g5 ♘e4!. In the Grünfeld, Black should always be looking for the most aggressive ideas, and never play passively. 5 ♗f4 ♘xc3 6 bxc3 ♗g7 7 e3 c5! continues in this spirit.

3) Black moves

Here we have 4 ♗f4 ♗g7 5 e3. Now 5...c5!? 6 dxc5 ♕a5! is a typical method. 7 ♖c1 can be met by 7...♘e4!? 8 cxd5 ♘xc3 9 ♕d2! or 7...dxc4 8 ♗xc4 0-0 9 ♘e2, with sharp play in both cases.

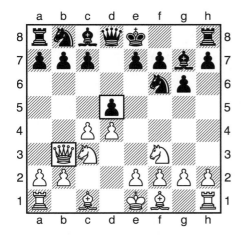

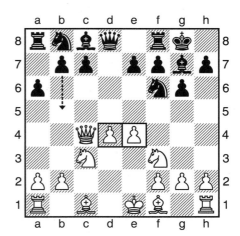

4) Black moves

The Russian System. Black's only active option is 5...dxc4 6 ♕xc4 0-0 7 e4, when White has a perfect pawn-centre, but an exposed queen. Black must strike back with all his might; one way is 7...a6 *(5)*.

5) White moves

The cunning point of this move is that White cannot prevent ...b5: after 8 a4? b5! 9 axb5? axb5 White loses rook or queen. But 8 e5 b5 9 ♕b3 ♘fd7 10 e6 fxe6 11 ♗e3 is much more testing.

Exchange Grünfeld

Grabbing all the space on offer

White accepts the invitation to set up a huge pawn-centre, and challenges Black to do his worst. After **1 d4 ♘f6 2 c4 g6 3 ♘c3 d5 4 cxd5 ♘xd5 5 e4 ♘xc3 6 bxc3 ♗g7** *(1a)*, there is no doubt that White's pawns are vulnerable (in particular the one on c3). They can also prove a mighty battering-ram: in the middlegame they provide cover for a kingside attack, and in the endgame they can swamp Black and create a winning passed pawn. Black must be highly vigilant, and make use of every scrap of counterplay and tactical opportunity that his active pieces can create. White used to play **7 ♗c4 c5 8 ♘e2** *(1b)* automatically, to avoid a pin by ...♗g4. Also the advance of White's f-pawn can be a powerful attacking idea. The lines after **8...♘c6 9 ♗e3 0-0 10 0-0** *(2)* are sharp and critical, but Black often benefits from the e2-knight's lack of control over e5. Therefore **7 ♘f3** has become popular. After **7...c5** *(3)*, the odd-looking **8 ♖b1 0-0 9 ♗e2** *(4)* simply removes targets from the long diagonal and gives Black complex problems.

Basic Positions of the Exchange Grünfeld

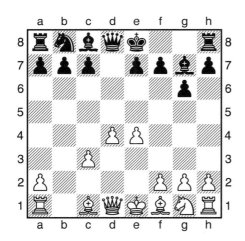

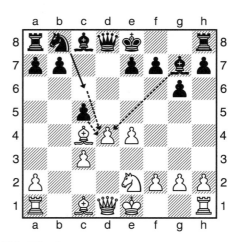

1a) White moves

White will support his centre with his pieces, keeping the pawns strong and mobile. Black will seek to break up and weaken White's pawn-centre.

1b) Black moves

After 8...♘c6, 9 d5 achieves little because 9...♘e5 gains time by threatening the bishop. 9 ♗e3 0-0 10 ♖c1, intending h4-h5, is an interesting attacking idea.

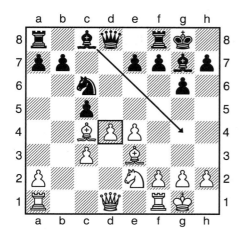

2) Black moves

10...♗g4 11 f3 ♘a5 starts an immediate battle. 12 ♗xf7+ wins a pawn that's not worth much. After 12 ♗d3 cxd4 13 cxd4 ♗e6 Black's grip on c4 can be broken by sacrificing a pawn with 14 ♖c1 ♗xa2, or an exchange by 14 d5!? ♗xa1 15 ♕xa1.

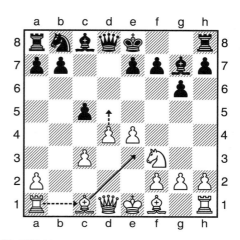

3) White moves

With the knight covering the e5-square, White's d5 advance is a real idea. After 8 ♗e3 ♕a5 9 ♕d2 ♘c6 10 ♖c1 (threatening d5!), Black should simplify by 10...cxd4 11 cxd4 ♕xd2+ 12 ♔xd2 0-0, when a complex ending lies ahead.

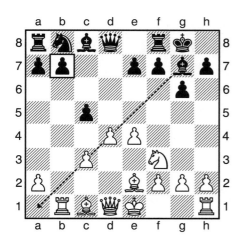

4) Black moves

The pressure on b7 deters 9...♗g4. After 9...♘c6 10 d5!, 10...♗xc3+ is a risky pawn-grab, and 10...♘e5 11 ♘xe5 ♗xe5 12 ♕d2 leads to sharp central play.

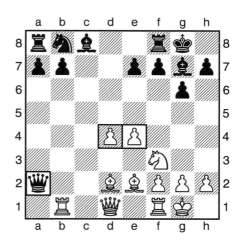

5) Black moves

The moves 9...cxd4 10 cxd4 ♕a5+ 11 ♗d2 ♕xa2 12 0-0 lead to this critical position. White has an ideal pawn-centre and Black has problems developing.

Queen's Indian and Bogo-Indian

Controlling the centre with pieces

After **1 d4 ♘f6 2 c4 e6**, White can avoid the Nimzo-Indian Defence (3 ♘c3 ♗b4 – see page 102) by playing **3 ♘f3**. Black has two unique plans, both leading to a manoeuvring game. First, he can play the popular **3...b6** *(1a)*, the Queen's Indian Defence. The idea is to follow up with ...♗b7 and control the long diagonal, particularly the critical d5- and e4-squares. White's most popular answer is to fianchetto his own bishop by 4 g3 ♗b7 5 ♗g2, when 5...♗e7 6 0-0 0-0 7 ♘c3 *(2)* usually follows. 4 ♘c3 immediately fights for e4 and d5. Then 4...♗b4 leads to Nimzo-Indian territory – we examine 5 ♗g5 on page 104. After 4...♗b7, one idea is 5 a3 *(3)*, preventing ...♗b4 and threatening 6 d5. Black can meet 5 ♗g5 with the solid 5...♗e7, or 5...h6!?. Black can also play **3...♗b4+** *(1b)*, the Bogo-Indian. If White blocks the check by 4 ♗d2, 4...♕e7 *(4)* protects the bishop. White sometimes prefers 4 ♘bd2 *(5)*, developing a piece and preparing 5 a3.

Basic Positions of the Queen's Indian and Bogo-Indian

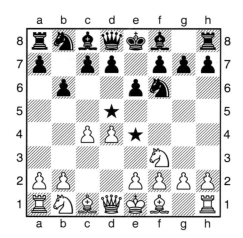
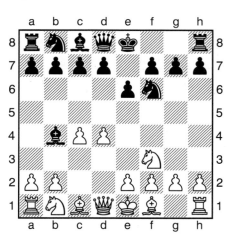

1a) White moves

Black controls the centre with his pieces and doesn't rush to put a pawn on the fourth rank. White will usually pursue a policy of central occupation. 4 g3 is a popular way to contest the long diagonal.

1b) White moves

Black gets his bishop out as quickly as possible, in order to get castled. If White plays 4 ♘c3, he's back in a Nimzo-Indian position (page 104), but he can also put a piece on d2 to block the check.

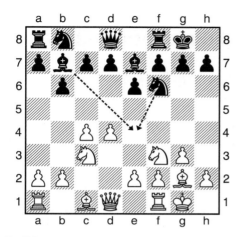

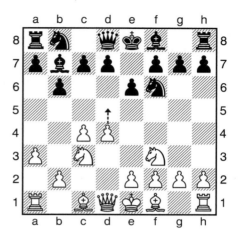

2) Black moves

White is ready to play 8 d5 or 8 ♕c2, to prepare e4. Black can cut off this plan at the pass by playing 7...♘e4, when he is ready to trade pieces and play either ...f5 or ...♗f6. Expect a slow game.

3) Black moves

5...♗e7? 6 d5! gives White a very firm grip on the centre, and leaves the b7-bishop poorly placed. 5...d5! grabs a share of the centre and can lead to positions similar to the Queen's Gambit Declined.

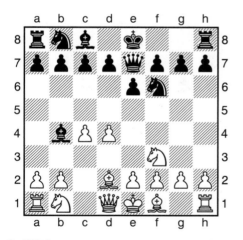

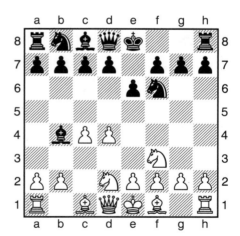

4) White moves

Now White should avoid 5 ♗xb4?! ♕xb4+ 6 ♕d2 ♘c6! 7 ♕xb4 ♘xb4. Then 8 ♔d1? allows 8...♘e4!, but the awkward 8 ♘a3 dooms the knight to a sad life on the edge of the board. 5 g3 ♘c6 6 ♘c3 is normal.

5) Black moves

White plans to play a3 next, either driving Black's powerful bishop back or exchanging it for the passive knight. Black has a lead in development after 4...0-0 and may play ...b6 and ...♗b7.

Nimzo-Indian: Introduction

Nimzowitsch's wonderful invention

1 d4 ♘f6 2 c4 e6 3 ♘c3 ♗b4 *(1a)* is the Nimzo-Indian Defence, perhaps the most complex opening in chess in terms of strategy. Black's first three moves aim for quick development (he's ready to castle) and control of the light squares e4 and d5. White will usually develop more slowly, but he often gets the bishop-pair and more space as compensation. These ideas appear following 4 a3 ♗xc3+ 5 bxc3 0-0 6 e3 c5 7 ♗d3 ♘c6 8 ♘e2 b6 9 e4 *(1b)*, as well as after 4 e3 c5 5 ♗d3 ♘c6 6 ♘f3 ♗xc3+ 7 bxc3 d6 8 e4 e5 *(2)*. Black wants to close the position and White can seek to crack it open by 9 d5 ♘e7 10 ♘h4 h6 11 f4 *(3)*. These lines can easily turn in Black's favour, thanks to his nimble knights. Another strategy has White moving his knight to e2 to defend the one on c3; for example, 4 e3 c5 5 ♘e2 cxd4 6 exd4 d5 7 a3 *(4)*. A similar idea is 4 e3 c5 5 ♗d3 d5 6 ♘e2 cxd4 7 exd4 *(5)*. This avoids doubled pawns, but the e2-knight can prove clumsy.

Basic Positions of the Nimzo-Indian

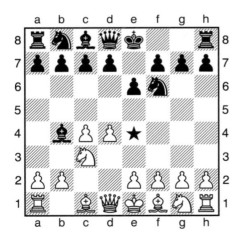

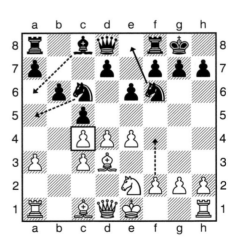

1a) White moves

White would like to construct a big mobile pawn-centre by playing e4 and perhaps f4. Black will try to stop this, first with pieces, but then with pawn moves (...e5, ...d5 or ...c5) if necessary.

1b) Black moves

Black intends to attack c4 with ...♗a6 and ...♘a5, while White tries to crash through to Black's king with f4, e5 and f5. To prevent this (and a pin by ♗g5), Black plays 9...♘e8 and ...f5 or ...f6.

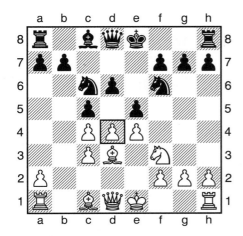

2) White moves

White needs to develop and open lines for his bishops. Black wants to block the centre since his knights will be strong in a closed position. 9 h3 h6 10 0-0 0-0 11 ♗e3 is a way to keep the central tension.

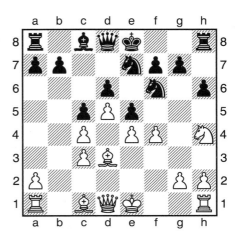

3) Black moves

White is trying to open the position, based upon the trick 11...exf4?! (the correct move is 11...♘g6!) 12 ♗xf4 g5?! 13 e5!, when no matter how Black captures, White's pieces spring to life.

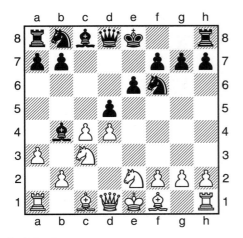

4) Black moves

7...♗xc3+ 8 ♘xc3 fails to double the white pawns. 7...♗e7!? leaves the knight in the way on e2. The simple 8 cxd5 ♘xd5 9 ♘xd5 ♕xd5 is comfortable for Black, but 8 ♘f4 is more ambitious.

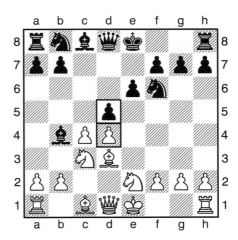

5) Black moves

Black will give White an isolated pawn after 7...dxc4 8 ♗xc4 or 7...♘c6 8 cxd5 ♘xd5 9 0-0 0-0. In both cases White has attacking chances, but Black can take aim at the vulnerable d4-pawn.

Nimzo-Indian: Main Lines

The opening that can go in any direction

The most popular line in the Nimzo-Indian is **1 d4 ♘f6 2 c4 e6 3 ♘c3 ♗b4 4 ♕c2** *(1a)*. White prevents doubled pawns (by ...♗xc3+). Now 4...0-0 5 a3 ♗xc3+ 6 ♕xc3 b6 7 ♗g5 ♗b7 *(1b)* is solid. By placing a bishop on b7, Black focuses on the key d5- and e4-squares. White's move ♗g5 brings his bishop in front of his pawns (compare 4 e3). If White wants a tactical game versus 4...0-0, he can play 5 e4, when 5...d5 6 e5 ♘e4 7 a3 ♗xc3+ 8 bxc3 c5 9 ♗d3 *(2)* leads to wild complications. Black can also play 4...d5 in response to 4 ♕c2. Then 5 cxd5 exd5 6 ♗g5 h6 7 ♗h4 *(3)* looks like a simple Queen's Gambit, but can get crazy. Another very popular move is 4 e3, when a traditional main line runs 4...0-0 5 ♗d3 d5 6 ♘f3 c5 7 0-0 ♘c6 8 a3 ♗xc3 9 bxc3 *(4)*. More dynamic is 4 ♘f3, when 4...c5 5 g3!? seeks to create pressure on the long h1-a8 diagonal, while 4...b6 5 ♗g5 ♗b7 6 e3 h6 7 ♗h4 g5 8 ♗g3 ♘e4 9 ♕c2 *(5)* leads to highly tense play.

Basic Positions of the Nimzo-Indian Main Lines

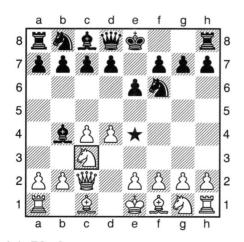

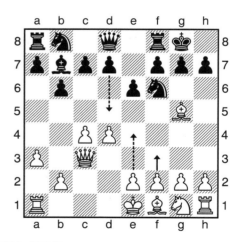

1a) Black moves

White covers e4 and avoids doubled c-pawns, but falls behind in development. Black has many possible responses, including the direct 4...d5, 4...c5 (attacking d4) and the flexible 4...0-0.

1b) White moves

Here 8 f3 intends 9 e4, but Black can stop that by 8...h6 9 ♗h4 d5. White still has the bishop-pair after 10 e3 ♘bd7, yet Black is happy to have the better development. Note 11 cxd5 ♘xd5!, exchanging queens.

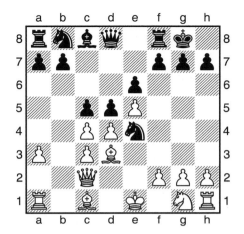

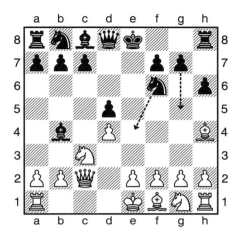

2) Black moves

A tactical paradise. The counterattack by 9...cxd4 10 cxd4 ♕a5+ provokes the complicated 11 ♔f1!. If 9...♕a5, lines like 10 ♘e2 cxd4 11 cxd5 exd5 12 f3! continue the fun.

3) Black moves

Black can play calmly, or try to bust things open by 7...c5 8 dxc5 g5 9 ♗g3 ♘e4 10 e3 ♕a5. Then 11 ♘e2 ♗f5 12 ♗e5!? 0-0 13 ♘d4 is a crazy position with all kinds of tactics ahead.

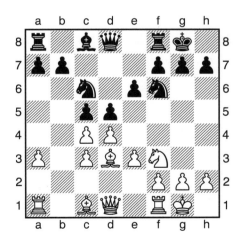

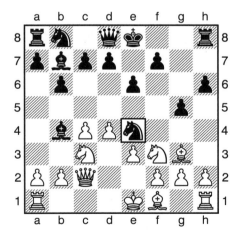

4) Black moves

As usual, White's two bishops are an asset, but he will have problems getting his queen's bishop out. The plan 9...dxc4 10 ♗xc4 ♕c7 prepares ...e5 and gives Black his fair share of the chances.

5) Black moves

9...♗xc3+ 10 bxc3 d6 11 ♗d3 gives White a poor pawn-structure but good central control. He opens lines after 11...♘xg3 12 fxg3!? or 11...f5 12 d5, at the cost of structure or material.

Reversed Sicilian

White plays Black and Black plays White

1 c4 is the English Opening. White intends to control the centre before occupying it, and may sit back and play a counterpunching game. A popular reply is **1...e5** *(1a)*, the Reversed Sicilian. Black is willing to give White an extra move over the Sicilian Defence (1 e4 c5), in spite of that opening's popularity. The two sides tend to bring out their forces cautiously, in preparation for later combat. Diagram 1b is a solid main line: 2 ♘c3 ♘f6 3 ♘f3 ♘c6 4 g3 ♗b4 5 ♗g2 0-0 6 0-0. Things can get more lively if Black deviates by 4...d5 5 cxd5 ♘xd5 6 ♗g2 *(2)*, a Reversed Dragon. White ends up with less space but better development in the variation 6...♘b6 7 0-0 ♗e7 8 d3 0-0 *(3)*. Sometimes White does without a fianchetto; for example, 4 e3 ♗b4 5 ♕c2 *(4)*. There are many other ways for both sides to develop, such as the frequently-played 'Botvinnik' structure, which is illustrated by 2 ♘c3 ♘c6 3 g3 g6 4 ♗g2 ♗g7 5 e4 ♘ge7 6 ♘ge2 0-0 7 0-0 d6 *(5)*.

Basic Positions of the Reversed Sicilian

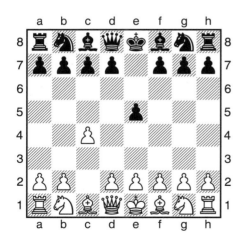

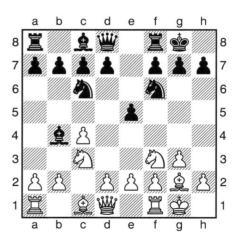

1a) White moves

Black has the 'white' side of the Sicilian with a move less. That should be OK, but he must avoid copying White's most aggressive systems from the Open Sicilian. They will not work a move down!

1b) Black moves

Black can expand by 6...e4 7 ♘g5 ♗xc3 8 bxc3 ♖e8. After White plays 9 f3, to activate his g2-bishop, Black has either the simple 9...exf3 or the gambit idea 9...e3!?, both producing wide-open play.

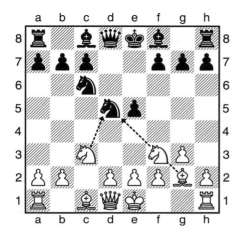

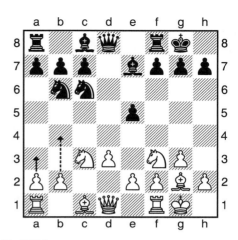

2) Black moves

This is a kind of reversed Dragon, with many of the same themes. But Black is a move behind and must be careful. 6...♗e7? loses a pawn to 7 ♘xe5!, with the idea 7...♘xc3 8 ♗xc6+ bxc6 9 dxc3.

3) White moves

White can be more ambitious than Black is in many Dragon variations by playing for queenside expansion with 9 a3 ♗e6 10 b4, followed by ♗b2, when his bishops bear down on the centre.

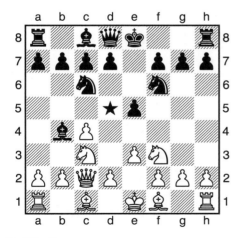

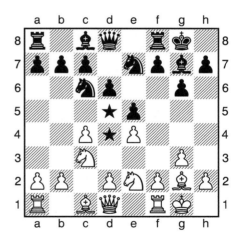

4) Black moves

Here 5...0-0 6 ♘d5 creates some problems, so Black might play for the centre by 5...♗xc3 6 ♕xc3 ♕e7, with 7...d5 next. White is still a couple of moves away from castling, so caution is needed.

5) White moves

White's pawns and pieces aim at d5, and Black has a potentially strong outpost on d4. A typical build-up of forces is 8 d3 ♗e6 9 ♘d5 f5 10 ♗e3 ♕d7. White can play for either the b4 or the f4 advance.

Symmetrical English

Anything you can do, I can do better

1 c4 c5 *(1a)* is called the Symmetrical English. Much as with 1 d4 d5 or 1 e4 e5, Black wants to confront White face on, and a common way to make progress is to advance a pawn to d4 (if White) or d5 (if Black). But there are a great many possible set-ups for both sides, sometimes with most or all of the bishops fianchettoed! In one traditional line, 1 c4 c5 2 ♘c3 ♘c6 3 ♘f3 ♘f6 4 g3 g6 5 ♗g2 ♗g7 6 0-0 0-0, White is first to the punch: 7 d4 *(1b)*. The move d4 can also appear earlier in this variation: 4 d4 cxd4 5 ♘xd4 e6 6 g3 *(2)*. Black can also play for ...d5 himself by answering 2 ♘c3 with 2...♘f6 3 ♘f3 d5 4 cxd5 ♘xd5, when 5 g3 ♘c6 6 ♗g2 ♘c7 *(3)* is one possibility, while a crazy-looking variation runs 5 e4 ♘b4 6 ♗c4 ♘d3+ *(4)*. In the line 2 ♘f3 ♘f6 3 g3 b6 4 ♗g2 ♗b7 5 ♘c3 e6 6 0-0 ♗e7 *(5)*, Black's formation is called the Hedgehog, because when White tries to attack it, he can easily get stung by his opponent's quills!

Basic Positions of the Symmetrical English

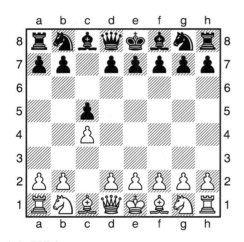

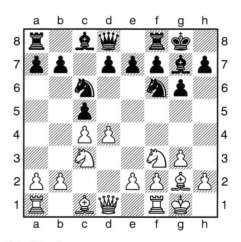

1a) White moves

In order to break symmetry, either White or Black can move his d-pawn two squares forward. The question is: when can this be done safely, without risking a strong counterattack?

1b) Black moves

Fearing 8 d5, Black cedes the centre by 7...cxd4 8 ♘xd4 ♘xd4 9 ♕xd4. White then controls more space, but after 9...d6 Black tries to get queenside play with ...♗e6 or ...a6 and ...b5.

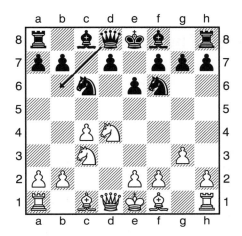

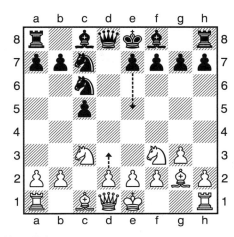

2) Black moves

White has more space, but this time Black develops with a series of forcing moves: 6...♕b6 7 ♘b3 ♘e5 8 e4 ♗b4. White defends the e4-pawn by 9 ♕e2 and prepares ♗e3 and f4, driving Black's pieces back.

3) White moves

Black has moved his knight three times, while White has developed quickly. But now ...e5 cannot be stopped, clamping down on the centre. The natural moves 7 0-0 e5 8 d3 ♗e7 can follow.

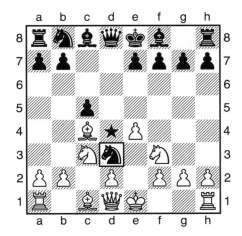

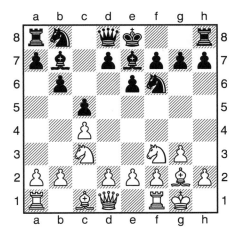

4) White moves

After 7 ♔e2! ♘f4+! 8 ♔f1, White threatens 9 d4, so Black resorts to a sixth move of his knight, 8...♘e6!, intending ...♘c6 and a take-over of d4. White's faster development gives him attacking chances.

5) White moves

White can grab space by 7 d4 cxd4 8 ♕xd4, but the apparently passive 8...d6 9 e4 ♘bd7 contains a drop of poison. In some lines, ...♘c5 and ...d5! will follow later. 7 ♖e1 plans e4 before playing d4.

Assorted English Lines

As long as the moves are logical, you can't go wrong

Since **1 c4** is a modest move, there's no need for Black to play a pawn to the fourth rank immediately. An obvious idea is **1...♘f6**, which might lead to structures from the Nimzo-Indian or King's Indian Defence. **2 ♘c3 e6 3 e4** *(1a)* firmly avoids the Nimzo-Indian and is called the Mikenas Attack. White contests d5, a goal put to the test after 3...d5 4 e5 d4 5 exf6 dxc3 6 bxc3 ♛xf6 7 d4 *(2)*. Black can also try to control d4 by 3...c5, when White often gambits a pawn with 4 e5 ♘g8 5 ♘f3 ♘c6 6 d4 cxd4 7 ♘xd4 ♘xe5 8 ♘db5 *(3)*. If Black sets up the King's Indian formation, a unique line called the Botvinnik System goes 2 ♘c3 g6 3 g3 ♗g7 4 ♗g2 0-0 5 e4 d6 6 ♘ge2 *(4)*. The eccentric English Defence begins **1...e6 2 d4 b6** *(1b)*. Highly original positions result, like 3 e4 ♗b7 4 ♘c3 ♗b4 5 ♛c2 ♛h4! *(5)*. 1...c6 leads to a Slav after 2 d4 d5, a Caro-Kann following 2 e4 d5 3 exd5 cxd5 4 d4, and a Réti (page 112) in the case of 2 ♘f3 d5.

Basic Positions of Assorted English Lines

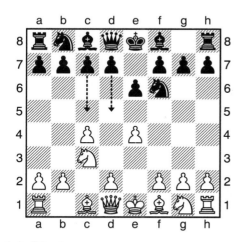

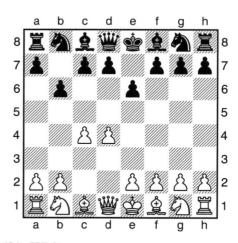

1a) Black moves

White occupies e4 and contests the d5-square. He avoids the Nimzo-Indian Defence, because 3...♗b4?! is strongly met by 4 e5!. Black has two better ways to confront 3 e4: 3...d5 and 3...c5.

1b) White moves

Black keeps his options open. He might play ...f5, ...c5 or ...d5, put his bishop on b4 or e7, and play ...♘e7 or ...♘f6. The main drawback is that White gets the lion's share of the centre.

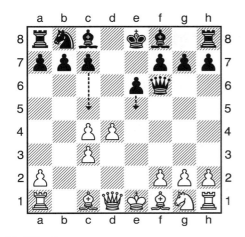

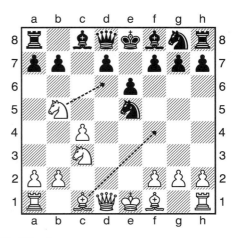

2) Black moves

Black has two ways to strike in the centre, but White replies energetically: 7...e5 8 ♘f3 exd4 9 ♗g5! or 7...c5 8 ♘f3 h6 (avoiding ♗g5!) 9 ♗d3 cxd4 10 cxd4 ♗b4+ 11 ♗d2 ♗xd2+ 12 ♕xd2 ♘c6.

3) Black moves

White has sacrificed a pawn to attack Black's dark squares. A main line goes 8...a6 9 ♘d6+ ♗xd6 10 ♕xd6 f6 11 ♗e3 ♘e7 12 ♗b6 ♘f5 13 ♕c5. Then White has pressure, but Black has an extra pawn.

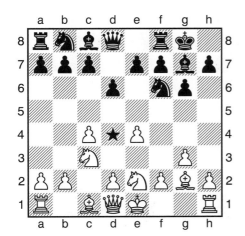

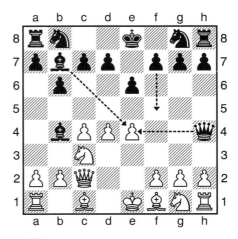

4) Black moves

This is similar to a position on page 107, but Black is flexible, and can deny White easy targets with set-ups like 6...c5 7 0-0 ♘c6 8 d3 a6 followed by ...♖b8 and ...b5 or 6...e5 7 0-0 c6 8 d3 a6, intending ...b5.

5) White moves

Strangely, both of Black's bishops and his queen come out before the knights! He is attacking e4, and 6 ♗d3 ♗xc3+ 7 bxc3 f5! continues Black's strategy of attacking the light squares.

111

Réti Opening

Watch out for attack from behind the lines

1 ♘f3 d5 2 c4 *(1a)* is the Réti Opening. In the main lines, White fianchettoes both bishops and uses their long range to attack Black's centre; e.g., 2...e6 3 b3 (3 g3 is also played, while 3 d4 is a Queen's Gambit Declined) 3...♘f6 4 ♗b2 ♗e7 5 g3 0-0 6 ♗g2 c5 7 0-0 ♘c6 8 e3 *(1b)*. 2...d4 can lead to more open play after 3 e3 ♘c6 4 exd4 ♘xd4. Black can also defend his pawn as he does in the Slav by 2...c6, when a typical set-up is 3 g3 (3 d4 is a regular Slav) 3...♘f6 4 ♗g2 ♗f5 5 b3 ♘bd7 6 ♗b2 e6 7 0-0 ♗d6 8 d3 0-0 *(2)*. There are some early tricks in the Réti Opening. For example, after 2...e6 3 b3 dxc4 4 bxc4 *(3)*, Black can seize a nice piece of the centre in one move.

What happens when Black decides to grab the c4-pawn? 2...dxc4 3 ♘a3 (3 e3 can transpose to a Queen's Gambit Accepted) 3...e5!? 4 ♘xe5 *(4)* involves two tricks. Also after 2...c6 3 g3 ♘f6 4 ♗g2 dxc4 5 ♕c2 b5 *(5)*, there is a sharp fight ahead.

Basic Positions of the Réti Opening

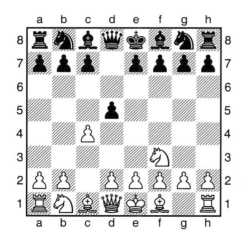

1a) Black moves
In the Réti Opening, Black sets up in the centre, and White attacks from the flanks, usually by putting his bishops on g2 and b2. This leads to a wonderful clash of chess philosophies.

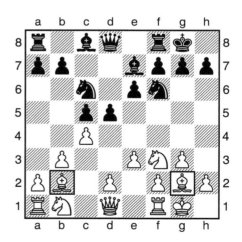

1b) Black moves
White's bishops aim at the four centre squares. Black can develop by 8...b6 and ...♗b7, or try to cramp White by 8...d4 9 exd4 cxd4. Then 10 ♖e1 prevents ...e5, which would sideline the b2-bishop.

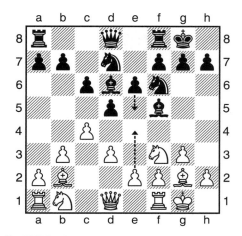

2) White moves

Again we see the fight between Black's central development and White's long-range pressure. Black usually expands in the centre with ...e5, while White can prepare e4 with ♘c3 or ♘bd2.

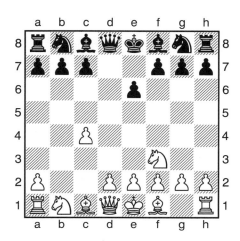

3) Black moves

Black looks passively placed without his d-pawn, but he can advance in the centre by 4...e5!, counting upon the fact that 5 ♘xe5?? loses a piece to 5...♕d4. 5 ♘c3 ♘c6 leads to more normal play.

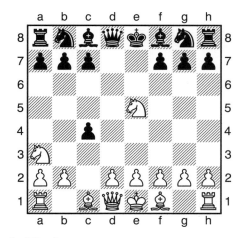

4) Black moves

At first sight, Black seems to win with the trick we just saw: 4...♗xa3 (intending 5 bxa3?? ♕d4), but White has 5 ♕a4+! ♘d7 (5...b5 6 ♕xa3 ♕d5 is another try) 6 ♘xd7 ♗xd7 7 ♕xa3 with good play.

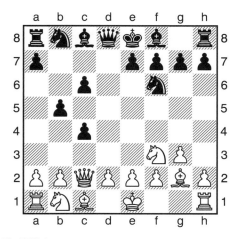

5) White moves

6 b3! cxb3 7 axb3 is an interesting gambit. White has active pieces and a target on c6. But Black is a pawn ahead and can allow White to win it back while he catches up with his own development.

Test Your Opening Knowledge

The time has come to put your opening knowledge to the test! Over the next 9 pages, you will be asked to name openings, give the moves that make up an opening, name opening positions, and tackle exercises that feature common opening tactics. You'll also have a chance to be an opening detective, and guess what opening a position came from. If you have read the book carefully, the first two pages should be a breeze...

Name the Opening

What name is given to each of the following openings?

1) 1 e4 e5 2 ♘f3 ♘c6 3 ♗b5
2) 1 e4 c5
3) 1 d4 d5 2 c4
4) 1 e4 e6
5) 1 d4 f5
6) 1 e4 e5 2 ♗c4
7) 1 e4 e5 2 ♘f3 ♘f6
8) 1 d4 ♘f6 2 c4 g6 3 ♘c3 d5
9) 1 d4 ♘f6 2 c4 c5 3 d5 b5
10) 1 e4 e5 2 ♘f3 f5
11) 1 e4 e5 2 ♘f3 ♘c6 3 ♗c4 ♗c5 4 b4
12) 1 d4 d5 2 c4 e6 3 ♘c3 c5
13) 1 ♘f3 d5 2 c4
14) 1 d4 ♘f6 2 c4 g6 3 ♘c3 ♗g7
15) 1 d4 d5 2 c4 c6 3 ♘f3 ♘f6 4 ♘c3 e6

Give the Moves

Write down the moves that match these opening names:

1) Two Knights Defence
2) King's Gambit
3) English Opening
4) Scandinavian Defence
5) Vienna Game
6) Giuoco Piano
7) Morra Gambit
8) Philidor Defence
9) Slav
10) Caro-Kann Defence
11) Alekhine Defence
12) Nimzo-Indian Defence
13) Scotch Game
14) Queen's Indian Defence
15) Sicilian Najdorf

HEDGEHOG

Name the Position

What opening variation is shown in each diagram?

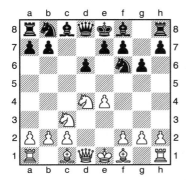

1) White to move

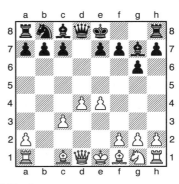

2) White to move

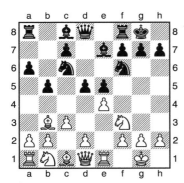

3) White to move

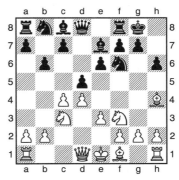

4) White to move

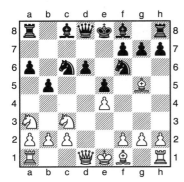

5) White to move

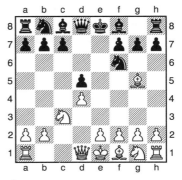

6) Black to move

115

Test Your Opening Skills

In each of the following 36 diagrams, you have two tasks:

1) Find the winning move for White or Black. Note that you are not necessarily looking for a forced checkmate – just a clear way to get a big advantage.

2) Identify the opening that has been played.

If you have read the book carefully, you should be able to work out many of the answers. Even though these exact positions have not occurred in the book so far, quite a lot (but not all!) of the ideas have been mentioned, or similar tactical traps have been highlighted. And in most cases, the pawn-structure should give you a strong clue about which opening was played.

If you are really stuck, then we have given a hint by telling you which section to consult. Of course, this removes part of the fun by telling you the opening name! The exercises start off easy, and get much harder.

Target Scores

Solutions begin on page 123. Give yourself 1 point for each opening correctly guessed *and* 1 point for each winning move found. You get only ½ point if you answered correctly after looking at the hint. Add your score to your number of correct answers from the Test Your Opening Knowledge section, to get a total out of 108.

100-108	**Master standard**
85-99	**Excellent club level**
70-84	**Very good opening skills**
50-69	**Promising opening ability**
31-49	**You'll impress them at the chess club!**
19-30	**You've learned a lot!**
0-18	**Oh dear! Try checkers?**

SYMMETRICAL ENGLISH

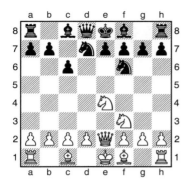

1) White wins
Hint: see Mighty Opening 17.

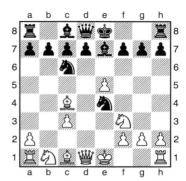

2) White wins
Hint: see Mighty Opening 2.

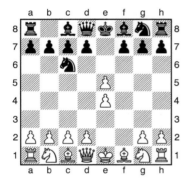

3) Black wins
Hint: see Mighty Opening 4.

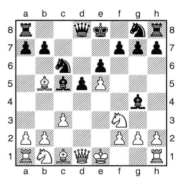

4) White wins
Hint: see Mighty Opening 17.

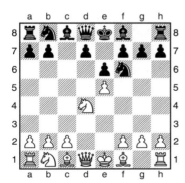

5) Black wins
Hint: see Mighty Opening 25.

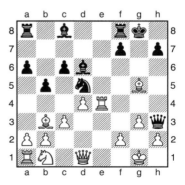

6) Black wins
Hint: see Mighty Opening 13.

117

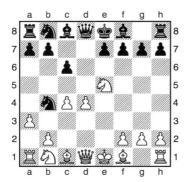

7) Black wins
Hint: see Mighty Opening 15.

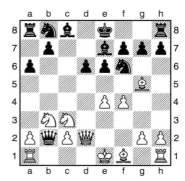

8) White wins
Hint: see Mighty Opening 27.

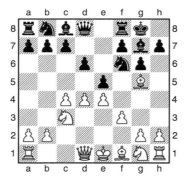

9) White wins
Hint: see Mighty Opening 40.

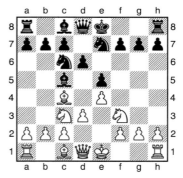

10) White wins
Hint: see Mighty Opening 1.

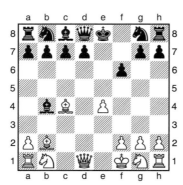

11) White wins
Hint: see Mighty Opening 5.

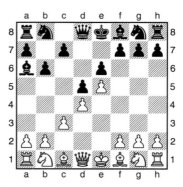

12) White wins
Hint: see Mighty Opening 18.

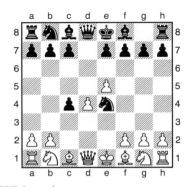

13) White wins
Hint: see Mighty Opening 29.

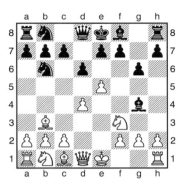

14) White wins
Hint: see Mighty Opening 15.

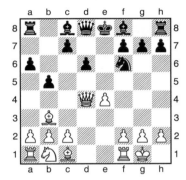

15) Black wins
Hint: see Mighty Opening 11.

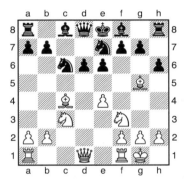

16) White wins
Hint: see Mighty Opening 23.

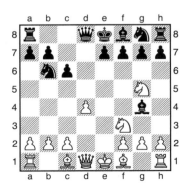

17) White wins
Hint: see Mighty Opening 17.

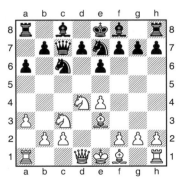

18) White wins
Hint: see Mighty Opening 25.

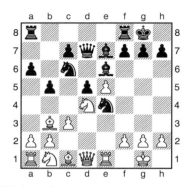

19) White wins
Hint: see Mighty Opening 14.

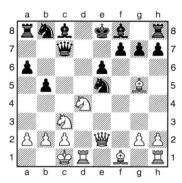

20) White wins
Hint: see Mighty Opening 27.

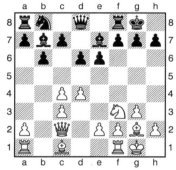

21) White wins
Hint: see Mighty Opening 44.

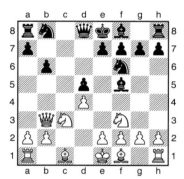

22) White wins
Hint: see Mighty Opening 35.

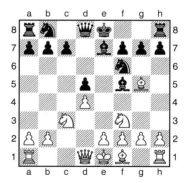

23) White wins
Hint: see Mighty Opening 32.

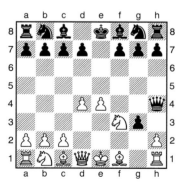

24) Black wins
Hint: see Mighty Opening 4.

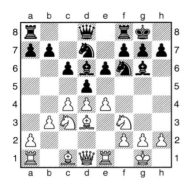

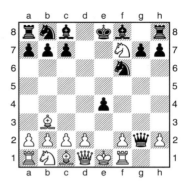

25) Black wins
Hint: see Mighty Opening 35.

26) Black wins
Hint: see Mighty Opening 6.

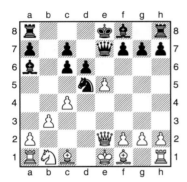

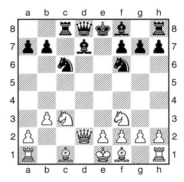

27) White wins
Hint: see Mighty Opening 8.

28) Black wins
Hint: see Mighty Opening 33.

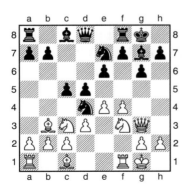

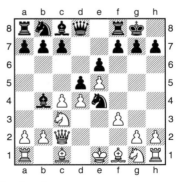

29) Black wins
Hint: see Mighty Opening 21.

30) Black wins
Hint: see Mighty Opening 46.

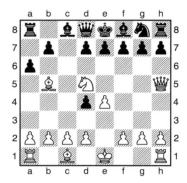

31) White wins
Hint: see Mighty Opening 24.

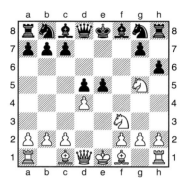

32) White wins
Hint: see Mighty Opening 9.

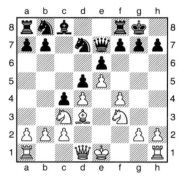

33) White wins
Hint: see Mighty Opening 19.

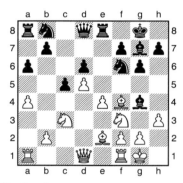

34) Black wins
Hint: see Mighty Opening 39.

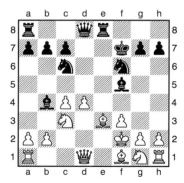

35) Black wins
Hint: see Mighty Opening 16.

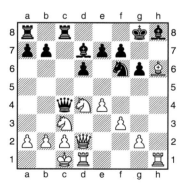

36) White wins
Hint: see Mighty Opening 26.

Test Solutions

FOUR KNIGHTS
GAME

Test Your Opening Knowledge

Name the Opening
1) Ruy Lopez
2) Sicilian Defence
3) Queen's Gambit
4) French Defence
5) Dutch Defence
6) Bishop's Opening
7) Petroff Defence
8) Grünfeld Defence
9) Benko Gambit
10) Latvian Gambit
11) Evans Gambit
12) Tarrasch Defence
13) Réti Opening
14) King's Indian Defence
15) Semi-Slav

Give the Moves
1) 1 e4 e5 2 ♘f3 ♘c6 3 ♗c4 ♘f6
2) 1 e4 e5 2 f4
3) 1 c4
4) 1 e4 d5
5) 1 e4 e5 2 ♘c3
6) 1 e4 e5 2 ♘f3 ♘c6 3 ♗c4 ♗c5
7) 1 e4 c5 2 d4 cxd4 3 c3
8) 1 e4 e5 2 ♘f3 d6
9) 1 d4 d5 2 c4 c6
10) 1 e4 c6
11) 1 e4 ♘f6
12) 1 d4 ♘f6 2 c4 e6 3 ♘c3 ♗b4

13) 1 e4 e5 2 ♘f3 ♘c6 3 d4
14) 1 d4 ♘f6 2 c4 e6 3 ♘f3 b6
15) 1 e4 c5 2 ♘f3 d6 3 d4 cxd4 4 ♘xd4 ♘f6 5 ♘c3 a6

Name the Position
1) **Sicilian Dragon** (1 e4 c5 2 ♘f3 d6 3 d4 cxd4 4 ♘xd4 ♘f6 5 ♘c3 g6)
2) **Exchange Grünfeld** (1 d4 ♘f6 2 c4 g6 3 ♘c3 d5 4 cxd5 ♘xd5 5 e4 ♘xc3 6 bxc3 ♗g7)
3) **Marshall Attack** (1 e4 e5 2 ♘f3 ♘c6 3 ♗b5 a6 4 ♗a4 ♘f6 5 0-0 ♗e7 6 ♖e1 b5 7 ♗b3 0-0 8 c3 d5)
4) **Tartakower Queen's Gambit** (1 d4 d5 2 c4 e6 3 ♘c3 ♘f6 4 ♗g5 ♗e7 5 e3 0-0 6 ♘f3 h6 7 ♗h4 b6)
5) **Sveshnikov Sicilian** (1 e4 c5 2 ♘f3 ♘c6 3 d4 cxd4 4 ♘xd4 ♘f6 5 ♘c3 e5 6 ♘db5 d6 7 ♗g5 a6 8 ♘a3 b5)
6) **Exchange Queen's Gambit** (1 d4 d5 2 c4 e6 3 ♘c3 ♘f6 4 cxd5 exd5 5 ♗g5)

Test Your Opening Skills

1. Black has carelessly fallen for White's crude threat: 6 ♘d6#.

Opening: Caro-Kann Defence: 1 e4 c6 2 ♘f3 d5 3 ♘c3 dxe4 4 ♘xe4 ♘d7 5 ♕e2 ♘gf6??.

2. 8 ♕d5 wins, as both 9 ♕xf7# and 9 ♕xe4 are threatened.

Opening: Evans Gambit: 1 e4 e5 2 Nf3 Nc6 3 Bc4 Bc5 4 b4 Bxb4 5 c3 Be7 6 d4 Nf6? 7 dxe5 Nxe4?.

3. 3...Qh4+ 4 g3 (or 4 Ke2 Qxe4+ 5 Kf2 Bc5+) 4...Qxe4+ 5 Qe2 Qxh1 and Black is a rook ahead.

Opening: King's Gambit: 1 e4 e5 2 f4 Nc6 3 fxe5??.

4. 8 Bxc6+! bxc6 9 Qa4!, threatening both Qxg4 and Qxc6+ followed by Qxc5+. Note that 8 Qa4? is ineffective due to 8...Bxf3 9 Qxc6+ Kf8!.

Opening: Caro-Kann Defence: 1 e4 c6 2 d4 d5 3 e5 c5 4 c3 Nc6 5 Nf3 Bg4 6 dxc5 e6 7 Bb5 Bxc5??.

5. 5...Qa5+ followed by ...Qxe5+ wins a pawn.

Opening: Open Sicilian: 1 e4 c5 2 Nf3 e6 3 d4 cxd4 4 Nxd4 Nf6 5 e5?.

6. 16...Qf5 wins a white piece, and is the justification for Black's 15th move (which prevented White's idea of 16 Rh4).

Opening: Ruy Lopez, Marshall Attack: 1 e4 e5 2 Nf3 Nc6 3 Bb5 a6 4 Ba4 Nf6 5 0-0 Be7 6 Re1 b5 7 Bb3 0-0 8 c3 d5 9 exd5 Nxd5 10 Nxe5 Nxe5 11 Rxe5 c6 12 d4 Bd6 13 Re1 Qh4 14 g3 Qh3 15 Re4 g5 16 Bxg5??.

7. 7...Qxd4! leaves Black a pawn up after 8 axb4 Qxe5+ or 8 Qxd4 Nc2+ and ...Nxd4, while the desperado 8 Nxf7 fails due to 8...Qe4+.

Opening: Alekhine Defence: 1 e4 Nf6 2 e5 Nd5 3 d4 d6 4 Nf3 dxe5 5 Nxe5 c6 6 c4 Nb4 7 a3?.

8. 10 a3 traps the black queen. Threats include Na4 and Ra2. 10 a4 is also good.

Opening: Sicilian Najdorf: 1 e4 c5 2 Nf3 d6 3 d4 cxd4 4 Nxd4 Nf6 5 Nc3 a6 6 Bg5 e6 7 f4 Qb6 8 Qd2 Qxb2 9 Nb3 Be7??.

9. White exchanges by 7 dxe5 dxe5 8 Qxd8 Rxd8 and now both 9 Bxf6 Bxf6 10 Nd5 and 9 Nd5 Nbd7 (or 9...Nxd5 10 Bxd8) 10 Nxc7 win material.

Opening: King's Indian Defence: 1 d4 Nf6 2 c4 g6 3 Nc3 Bg7 4 e4 d6 5 f3 0-0 6 Bg5 e5??.

10. 6 Ng5! d5 (6...0-0? 7 Qh5 h6 8 Nxf7) 7 exd5 Na5 8 Qh5 g6 9 Qe2 with an extra pawn and strong attack.

Opening: Giuoco Piano: 1 e4 e5 2 Nf3 Nc6 3 Bc4 Bc5 4 d3 d6 5 Nc3 Nge7?.

11. Black's last move (...f6) prevented Bxg7, but allowed 7 Bxg8 (7 Qb3 is also good) 7...Rxg8 8 Qb3 Rf8 9 Qxb4.

Opening: Danish Gambit: 1 e4 e5 2 d4 exd4 3 c3 dxc3 4 Bc4 cxb2 5 Bxb2 Bb4+ 6 Kf1 f6??.

12. 5 Bxa6 (not 5 Qa4+? Qd7) 5...Nxa6 6 Qa4+ wins a piece. Black's idea of exchanging off his 'bad' bishop was strategically a good idea, but failed tactically here.

Opening: French Defence: 1 e4 e6 2 d4 d5 3 e5 b6 4 c3 Ba6??.

13. 5 f3 traps Black's knight in the middle of the board!

Opening: Queen's Gambit Accepted: 1 d4 d5 2 c4 dxc4 3 e4 Nf6 4 e5 Ne4?.

14. 7 ♗xf7+! ♔xf7 8 ♘g5+ followed by ♕g4 wins a pawn and leaves Black's position in ruins.

Opening: Alekhine Defence: 1 e4 ♘f6 2 e5 ♘d5 3 d4 d6 4 ♘f3 g6 5 ♗c4 ♘b6 6 ♗b3 ♗g4??.

15. 9...c5 followed by ...c4 wins the white bishop. This is the Noah's Ark Trap.

Opening: Ruy Lopez: 1 e4 e5 2 ♘f3 ♘c6 3 ♗b5 a6 4 ♗a4 d6 5 0-0 ♘f6 6 d4 b5 7 ♗b3 ♘xd4 8 ♘xd4 exd4 9 ♕xd4??.

16. The alert 9 ♘b5! wins. After 9...d5 one way through for White is 10 ♗f4 ♘g6 11 ♗c7 ♕d7 12 exd5 exd5 13 ♖e1+ ♗e7 14 ♘d6+ ♔f8 15 ♕xd5.

Opening: Morra Gambit: 1 e4 c5 2 d4 cxd4 3 c3 dxc3 4 ♘xc3 ♘c6 5 ♘f3 d6 6 ♗c4 e6 7 0-0 ♘ge7 8 ♗g5 h6??.

17. 7 ♘xf7 wins in view of 7...♔xf7 8 ♘e5+ and ♕g4, while 7...♗xf3 doesn't help since 8 ♕xf3 defends the f7-knight.

Opening: Caro-Kann Defence: 1 e4 c6 2 d4 d5 3 ♘d2 dxe4 4 ♘xe4 ♘d7 5 ♘g5 ♘b6 6 ♘1f3 ♗g4??.

18. 8 ♘db5! takes advantage of the black king and queen's lack of space. After 8...axb5 9 ♘xb5 ♕b8 (9...♕a5+ 10 b4 doesn't help) 10 ♘d6+ ♔d8 11 ♗b6+, Black's queen is lost.

Opening: Open Sicilian: 1 e4 c5 2 ♘f3 e6 3 d4 cxd4 4 ♘xd4 ♘c6 5 ♘c3 a6 6 ♗e3 ♕c7 7 a3 ♘ge7??.

19. After 12 ♘xe6!, Black loses a piece one way or another due to a pin: 12...♕xe6 13 ♖xe4 or 12...fxe6 13 ♖xe4.

20. 12 ♘dxb5! wins because 12...axb5 13 ♕xe5! ♕xe5 14 ♖d8# is mate.

Opening: Sicilian Najdorf: 1 e4 c5 2 ♘f3 d6 3 d4 cxd4 4 ♘xd4 ♘f6 5 ♘c3 a6 6 ♗g5 e6 7 f4 b5 8 e5 dxe5 9 fxe5 ♕c7 10 ♕e2 ♘fd7 11 0-0-0 ♘xe5??.

21. 10 ♘g5! ♗xg5 (not 10...♗xg2? 11 ♕xh7#) 11 ♗xb7 and White will end up with a rook for a piece.

Opening: Queen's Indian Defence: 1 d4 ♘f6 2 c4 e6 3 ♘f3 b6 4 g3 ♗b7 5 ♗g2 ♗e7 6 0-0 0-0 7 ♘c3 ♘e4 8 ♕c2 ♘xc3 9 bxc3 d6?.

22. White has several strong moves here, but 7 e4! dxe4 8 ♘e5 is the most direct. Black is in deep trouble after 8...e6 9 ♗b5+ ♘fd7 10 g4 ♗g6 11 h4 or 8...♗e6 9 ♗b5+ ♘fd7 10 d5 ♗f5 11 ♗g5! intending d6 and ♘d5, with an overwhelming attack; e.g., 11...f6 12 d6 e6 13 g4 or 11...a6 12 d6 ♗e6 13 ♘d5. If you saw 7 e4! and the main ideas, then consider the exercise solved.

Opening: Slav: 1 d4 d5 2 c4 c6 3 ♘f3 ♘f6 4 ♘c3 ♗f5?! 5 cxd5 cxd5?! 6 ♕b3 b6?.

23. 7 ♗xf6! ♗xf6 8 ♕b3! wins either the b7-pawn or the d5-pawn. 7 ♕b3!? ♘bd7 is good for White, though slightly less clear.

Opening: Queen's Gambit Declined: 1 d4 d5 2 c4 e6 3 ♘c3 ♘f6 4 cxd5 exd5 5 ♗g5 ♗e7 6 ♘f3 ♗f5?.

24. 5...g2+! 6 ♘xh4 gxh1♕ and Black is a rook and pawn ahead.

Opening: King's Gambit: 1 e4 e5 2 f4 exf4 3 d4?! ♕h4+ 4 g3?? fxg3 5 ♘f3.

25. White's central advance is poorly supported, and after 10...♗b4! he loses material.

Opening: Slav: 1 d4 d5 2 c4 c6 3 ♘f3 ♘f6 4 e3 ♗f5 5 ♗d3 ♗g6 6 ♘c3 e6 7 0-0 ♗d6 8 b3 ♘bd7 9 ♖e1 0-0 10 e4??.

26. 8...♗g4 9 f3 ♗xf3 10 ♖xf3 exf3 and White can't stop ...f2+ and ...f1♕++ without giving up his queen.

Opening: Latvian Gambit: 1 e4 e5 2 ♘f3 f5 3 ♗c4 fxe4 4 ♘xe5 ♕g5 5 ♘f7?! ♕xg2 6 ♖f1 d5 7 ♗xd5 ♘f6 8 ♗b3??.

27. 10 ♕e4! wins a pawn after 10...♘b6 11 ♕xc6+, because if Black instead plays 10...♘b4?, 11 a3 traps his knight!

Opening: Scotch Game: 1 e4 e5 2 ♘f3 ♘c6 3 d4 exd4 4 ♘xd4 ♘f6 5 ♘xc6 bxc6 6 e5 ♕e7 7 ♕e2 ♘d5 8 c4 ♗a6 9 b3 d6?.

28. 10...♗b4! 11 ♗b2 (11 ♕e3+ ♘e7! 12 ♗d2 ♗xc3 13 ♗xc3 ♘d5 and Black wins a piece) 11...♘e4 12 ♕e3 ♗f5!, winning. Black threatens not only ...♗c5, but also ...♕a5 and ...♘e7, both winning a piece.

Opening: Tarrasch Defence: 1 d4 d5 2 c4 e6 3 ♘c3 c5 4 cxd5 cxd4 5 ♕xd4 ♘c6 6 ♕d1 exd5 7 ♕xd5 ♗d7 8 ♘f3 ♘f6 9 ♕d2?! ♖c8 10 b3?.

29. 10...c4! and Black wins a piece after both 11 ♗a4 b5 12 ♗xb5 ♘xb5 13 ♘xb5 ♕b6+ and 11 dxc4 dxc4 12 ♗xc4 ♘xf3+ followed by ...♕d4+.

30. 7...♕h4+ 8 g3 (8 ♔d1 ♘f2+ 9 ♔e2 ♘xh1) 8...♘xg3! 9 ♕f2 (9 hxg3 ♕xh1) 9...♘f5 and Black remains a pawn ahead.

Opening: Nimzo-Indian Defence: 1 d4 ♘f6 2 c4 e6 3 ♘c3 ♗b4 4 ♕c2 0-0 5 e4 d5 6 e5 ♘e4 7 f3?.

31. 8 ♕e5! wins: 8...f6 (after 8...e6 9 ♘c7+ White wins material) 9 ♘c7+ ♔f7 10 ♕d5+ e6 (10...♔g6 11 ♘e6!) 11 ♘xe6!.

Opening: ♗b5 Sicilian: 1 e4 c5 2 ♘f3 ♘c6 3 ♗b5 ♕b6 4 ♘c3 ♘d4?! 5 ♘xd4 cxd4 6 ♘d5 ♕d8 7 ♕h5! a6??.

32. 7 ♘f7! ♔xf7 8 ♘xe5+ ♔e8 9 ♕h5+ ♔e7 10 ♘g6+, winning material. A tricky idea, but the opening was probably even harder to guess...

Opening: Philidor Defence: 1 e4 e5 2 ♘f3 d6 3 d4 f5?! 4 ♘c3 fxe4?! 5 ♘xe4 d5?! 6 ♘eg5! h6?.

33. A standard 'Greek Gift' sacrifice works well here: 10 ♗xh7+! ♔xh7 11 ♘g5+ ♔g6 (11...♔g8? 12 ♕h5 leads to checkmate unless Black gives up his queen by 12...♕xg5) 12 ♕g4 f5 13 ♕g3 ♘c6 14 ♘xe6+ ♔h6 15 ♕h3+ ♔g6 16 g4! fxg4 (16...♕xe6 17 ♕h5#) 17 ♕xg4+ ♔f7 18 f5! with a huge attack – and White already has two pawns for his piece and will pick up more material.

Opening: French Defence: 1 e4 e6 2 d4 d5 3 ♘c3 ♘f6 4 ♗g5 ♗e7 5 e5 ♘fd7 6 ♗xe7 ♕xe7 7 f4 0-0 8 ♘f3 c5 9 ♗d3 c4?.

34. 12...♘xe4! wins a pawn thanks to some neat tactics. The main idea is 13 hxg4 ♗xc3 14 bxc3? ♘xc3 and ...♘xe2+, while after 13 ♘xe4 ♖xe4 14 ♗g5 (14 hxg4 ♖xf4) 14...♕e8! 15 ♗d3 (15 hxg4 ♖xe2) 15...♗xf3 16 ♕xf3 ♖b4 Black stays a pawn ahead.

Opening: Modern Benoni: 1 d4 ♘f6 2 c4 c5 3 d5 e6 4 ♘c3 exd5 5 cxd5 d6 6 e4 g6 7 ♘f3 ♗g7 8 ♗e2 0-0 9 0-0 a6 10 a4 ♗g4 11 ♗f4 ♖e8 12 h3?.

35. 10...♖xe3! 11 ♔xe3 ♗c2!! and White loses his queen in view of 12 ♕xc2 ♕xd4+ 13 ♔e2 ♗xc3 and ...♖e8+, or 12 ♕d2 ♘g4+! 13 fxg4 (13 ♔e2 ♕e7+) 13...♕g5+ 14 ♔e2 ♖e8+.

Opening: Scandinavian Defence: 1 e4 d5 2 exd5 ♘f6 3 d4 ♗g4 4 f3 ♗f5 5 c4 e6 6 dxe6 ♘c6 7 exf7+? ♔xf7 8 ♗e3 ♗b4+ 9 ♔f2 ♖e8 10 ♘c3?.

36. 17 ♗f8!! ♖xf8 18 ♖xh8+! ♔xh8 19 ♕h6+ ♔g8 20 ♘d5! and Black has no viable defence; e.g., 20...♖fe8 21 ♘xf6+ exf6 22 ♖h1 ♗h3 23 ♖xh3 or 20...♘xd5 21 ♖h1! ♗h3!? 22 ♘f5!. This is a very difficult idea to find. Very well done if you succeeded. If not, maybe you had better luck guessing the opening...

Opening: Sicilian Dragon: 1 e4 c5 2 ♘f3 d6 3 d4 cxd4 4 ♘xd4 ♘f6 5 ♘c3 g6 6 ♗e3 ♗g7 7 f3 ♘c6 8 ♕d2 0-0 9 ♗c4 ♗d7 10 0-0-0 ♕c7 11 ♗b3 ♖fc8 12 h4 ♘e5 13 ♗h6 ♗h8?! 14 h5 ♘c4 15 hxg6! hxg6? 16 ♗xc4 ♕xc4.

NOAH'S ARK TRAP

127

Conclusion

OK, it's time to put your knowledge to use. The only way to really master the opening (and chess) is to play a lot of games. When you do that, be sure to take notation, that is, write down the moves as you play. Try using an opening that appeals to you, and when you finish the game, whether you win or lose, go back and think about how you played the opening. Check with this book to see where the moves of your game differed from those that we've shown, and try to figure out what you would do to improve your play if the same position came up in a future game. As you compete more and more, you'll get better at spotting both your mistakes and those of your opponents.

You can also learn a lot from working with a computer – and there is a lot of good free material available on the Internet, such as database programs (e.g., ChessBase Light), game downloads (e.g., The Week In Chess) and freeware analysis engines. Use a database program to find recent games in the openings you like, and really try to understand why the grandmasters are putting their pieces on particular squares. An analysis engine will help explain tactical decisions, and can be used to test your own ideas.

Once you become seriously involved in tournaments, you'll probably want to get specialized books on at least some of the openings you play. A good book can provide insights and ideas that you'd be hard-pressed to discover from your own research. If you play complicated openings at more advanced levels, you will also end up having to memorize some variations, just because they would take too long to work out completely in the heat of battle. But in the end, most of what you do will come down to closer and better application of the principles and techniques we've emphasized in this book. If you've got those down, you will be able to play any opening with confidence, and even invent new opening variations of your own!

King's Indian Defence